Year One in Action

Children are 'hard-wired' to learn and they learn best by being active and autonomous – exploring, discovering, creating and taking risks; in other words, by playing. However, formal, subject-specific lessons and a focus on data, targets and unrealistic expectations are causing young children to be bored and stressed and this is stifling their learning. *Year One in Action* reveals the remarkable progress children can make when they are allowed to pursue their own interests, ideas and challenges in a superb and enabling environment supported by responsive, skilled and empathic staff.

Demonstrating how a child-led approach supports the development of purposeful, calm, confident and independent children, this book offers a unique month-by-month insight into the workings of a highly successful Year One class. It covers all aspects of practice from timetabling, adult roles and transitions, to the organisation of the classroom and outside area. It tracks the events of each month in the year, paying close attention to the physical environment and the learning that is taking place. Interactions between staff and children are recognised as, and exploited as, teaching opportunities. Throughout the book, Anna Ephgrave gives the reasons behind each decision made. She also explains what the outcomes have been for the children, emphasising that a child-led approach, with planning in the moment, enables rich learning across the curriculum for all children within a meaningful context.

Key features include:

- over 150 full colour photographs to illustrate practice;
- photocopiable pages of planning sheets, record keeping sheets, sample letters to parents;
- examples of individual learning journeys and planning 'in the moment';
- guidance on what to look for when assessing children's progress;
- advice on risk/benefit assessments;
- suggestions for managing transitions and minimising stress.

The achievements of these children have been remarkable and they have remained the enthusiastic, independent, happy and unique individuals that they were when they came into Year One. Written by a leading consultant teacher, this book will inspire teachers to be brave and do what is right for children – let them take the lead, trust that they want to learn and above all let them play!

Anna Ephgrave has been teaching for over 27 years. Her most recent post was Assistant Head Teacher responsible for the Early Years and Year One at Carterhatch Infant School, which was graded as Outstanding in its most recent inspection. Anna is an independent consultant, trainer and author, supporting practitioners both in the United Kingdom and abroad. She has written two very successful books for David Fulton, Routledge: *The Reception Year in Action* and *The Nursery Year in Action*.

Year One in Action

A Month-by-Month Guide to Taking Early Years Pedagogy into KS1

Anna Ephgrave

Routledge
Taylor & Francis Group

LONDON AND NEW YORK

First published 2017
by Routledge
2 Park Square, Milton Park, Abingdon, Oxon OX14 4RN

and by Routledge
711 Third Avenue, New York, NY 10017

Routledge is an imprint of the Taylor & Francis Group, an informa business

British Library Cataloguing in Publication Data
A catalogue record for this book is available from the British Library

Library of Congress Cataloging in Publication Data
Names: Ephgrave, Anna, author.
Title: Year one in action : a month-by-month guide to success in the classroom / Anna Ephgrave.
Description: Abingdon, Oxon ; New York, NY : Routledge, [2017] | Includes bibliographical
references.
Identifiers: LCCN 2016041451 | ISBN 9781138639218 (hardback) |
ISBN 9781138639256 (pbk.) | ISBN 9781315637327 (ebook)
Subjects: LCSH: First grade (Education)—Curricula. | First grade (Education)—
Activity programs.
Classification: LCC LB1571 1st .E65 2017 | DDC 372.19—dc23
LC record available at https://lccn.loc.gov/2016041451

ISBN: 978-1-138-63921-8 (hbk)
ISBN: 978-1-138-63925-6 (pbk)
ISBN: 978-1-315-63732-7 (ebk)

Typeset in Bembo
by Keystroke, Neville Lodge, Tettenhall, Wolverhampton

Contents

Foreword

It gives me enormous pleasure to write this Foreword. Anna's two other publications (*The Reception Year in Action* and *The Nursery Year in Action*) have impacted so many settings, practitioners and children, showing exactly how to run the true early years approach. It is fantastic to see this approach now being showcased in Year One and how successful it is in ensuring children learn about the world, themselves and the basics of education.

This book follows the pursuits of a class of Year One children over the course of a year as they experience the true early years approach. The true early years approach involves interested adults, who know their children; all their children, not just some of them. Adults who understand that the reason anyone (not just children) learns anything is because they are interested and keen. They know that people learn by trial and error, practice, redesigning/rewriting/redrawing. For example, when I get my new phone from its box I will push buttons, turn it around, look all about it to find out how it works, find out what its potential is and then I will read the instructions and follow those and give it a go. This is playing. If adults learn in this way then surely children need experience of giving something a go, creating and recreating and making mistakes? And this is what this book makes so clear – it discusses and shares children playing and this is not considered an 'early years' or a childish approach, but as the driving force of success for everyone, including children.

Throughout you can see this child-centred approach working so well for the children. Anna Ephgrave makes crystal clear what play is and its centrality to young children's learning and development. The book is full of wonderful images of real children concentrating in their play and being happy. Through these images and the writing, one views the set-up of the environment both inside and out to ensure these children are facilitated in their keenness to play and learn.

This is such an important book because these Year One children are doing the early years approach and gosh, they are being highly successful! Sadly this is not the norm in Key Stage One with pressure often placed on children from a formal, adult-led approach. It is a breath of fresh air to see these children learning in a developmentally appropriate way in an environment that enables them to explore, discover, create and take risks supported by knowledgeable and understanding adults. These children are reading and writing and talking and listening and caring and picking themselves up when they make a mistake and helping one another. They are persevering independently, not with anyone at their backs; they are imagining and considering and then going and seeking solutions. Not because someone has told them, but because they want to!

Everyone in education should read this book, because this is how education should be! What an inspiration the staff and children are at Carterhatch school. I thank you for the work you are doing.

Dr Helen Bilton
September 2016

Acknowledgements

Over ten years ago, Ruth Moore became the Early Years Strategy Manager for the London Borough of Enfield, where I was a team leader. Ruth influenced many people during the six years that she was in post, and thousands of children benefited from the practice that she encouraged. She is an enabler, supporting and facilitating practitioners to be the best they can be. She invited Helen Bilton to visit my school and Helen encouraged me to write my first book. So I must thank both Ruth and Helen for having such belief in me and pushing me to do things that have changed my life.

In order to write this (my third) book, I needed the support of my head teacher and so I must thank Andrew Boyes who was instrumental in setting up the Year One practice at Carterhatch Infant School, before he moved to his new job in Islington. He has been replaced by joint head teachers, Adrienne Barrell and Sarah Clements, who are equally committed to child-led learning and have supported the work in Year One. As new head teachers, this was a brave thing to do and I thank them for this leap of faith. The children have benefited enormously and their joyful faces, throughout this book, illustrate their gratitude.

My role in the school is an assistant head teacher, so I do not have responsibility for a class. Clearly, this book would not have been possible without the hard work and commitment of the staff team. In particular, I must thank Jacqui Granger who has been the lead teacher in Year One this year and she has organised and motivated the team to work relentlessly to make the year a success. We have met on numerous occasions through the year, along with the other teachers, and, as with my previous books, her contribution has been invaluable. In September there were two other teachers in post – Ruth Richards and Rachel Walker. Both spent many hours with myself and Jacqui, agreeing the vision, discussing progress, sorting photos, collating information and celebrating the wonderful outcomes. Ruth went on maternity leave in January and Jo Jenkins and Lynn Sodoli took her place, stepping in and carrying on to make a seamless transition for the children. So I thank all these teachers – Jacqui, Ruth, Rachel, Jo and Lynn. They have not been alone in Year One. We are incredibly lucky to have learning support assistants as well. Visitors to the school cannot tell who are the teachers and who are the learning support assistants. This is testament to their skill and dedication. They have worked so hard and my thanks cannot reflect my true gratitude to them. So I thank Alice Jenner, Charlene Williams, Tas Begum, Yesim Hussein, Marie L'aiguille and Katya Jenkins.

Of course, as with my other books, the biggest thanks must go to the children and their families. Thank you again for being you! It has been such a privilege to see this group of children grow and develop through nursery, Reception and now Year One. The documentation of their journey is being shared across the world. Teachers are sharing the experiences of Carterhatch children and learning that education can be engaging and enjoyable. I get messages every week from teachers, thanking me for these books, but their gratitude should be directed to everyone involved, especially the children. So thank you all!

Jacqui and her daughter Kara, 19 September 2016

Introduction

Pedagogy

At Carterhatch, we have found a way to ensure that every one of the 90 children in Year One has access to an education that is uniquely suited to them as individual learners, where they are also becoming co-operative and responsible members of the school society. They are equipped with the literacy and maths skills that they need in order to 'play' and learn about the things that interest them. Through this they have thrived – their achievements have been remarkable, while they have remained the enthusiastic, independent, happy and unique individuals that they were when they came into Year One. Children aged five or six want to learn. Moreover, they want to be active, autonomous and unique learners – exploring, discovering, creating and taking risks. In other words they want to **play**. They each have different life histories, leading to unique personalities, interests, needs and skills. But they all want to **play** in order to satisfy their desire to learn. However, in many schools Year One feels like secondary school, with formal, subject-specific lessons and an approach that implies 'one size fits all'. For many children the size is wrong, the children are bored and stressed and their desire to learn has been extinguished. The curriculum in many such schools has been narrowed down to virtually nothing but literacy and maths – as if these subjects are an end in themselves, rather than tools that can lead to exciting learning in infinite areas. This is a tragedy for the five and six year old children in England.

Some readers may already be losing interest, thinking 'Oh she's talking about **play**'. However, let me stress that **play** can mean many things but for the purposes of this book **'play is whatever a child does in order to satisfy their desire to learn'**. As such, **play is a serious business**. The child who needs a light for the top of their robot will persevere with the wires, batteries and bulbs until they achieve success – **this is play**. The child who wants to traverse the complete run of monkey bars will stay outside for three hours trying different techniques – **this is play**. The child who wants the basketball net fixed will sit for a long period, writing a polite and clear letter to persuade the site staff to come and help – **this is play**. The child who wants to make pizza with only limited funds will discuss, read and research to make sure the result will be tasty – **this is play**. These are in fact just a tiny sample of the real examples of learning through play that I witnessed in Year One in just one morning this week. Imagine what you will discover when reading about the whole year that is described in the rest of this book!

In these, and every other example in the book, no one has told the children what, where, when or how to play. They have been pursuing their own interests, ideas and challenges in a superb enabling environment supported by responsive, skilled, empathic staff. Each day there are short, direct, adult-led teaching slots for reading, phonics and maths. These slots are timetabled at the start and end of the morning or afternoon sessions, so that there are still long periods during which the children can get deeply involved in their play – applying their literacy and maths skills where appropriate, in order to further their learning. The staff constantly reflect on and review the timetable, the environment and their role in order to maximise learning. However, the underlying pedagogy is this:

Children are born with a natural desire to explore and learn and we, the adults, support them by creating an enabling environment and through the relationships and interactions that the children experience. **We do not plan ahead**, rather we remain '**in the moment**' with the children as they explore and learn. We observe carefully, and enhance the learning whenever we spot a 'teachable moment'. Some of our observations, interactions and the outcomes are recorded afterwards.

This is a simple message – **let the children choose what to do, join them and support them in their pursuits and then write up a selection of what has happened**. The rest of this book will explain in detail how this looks in practice and what outcomes are achieved.

Brain development and progress

When a person learns something, new synapses form in the brain – this is progress. When a child is deeply engaged in their play – persevering to master a new skill, summoning the courage to stretch to the next rung on the ladder, arguing their point to a friend, cutting a shape with great precision, calculating the total cost of the items they wish to buy – in this state, new synapses are forming, learning is occurring and progress is happening. This is the state that children naturally want to be in. **Children do not want to be bored**. If they are bored, they will look for something else to do that is more interesting – even if this means they get into trouble! Thus I see behaviour issues arise in many schools, for example during lengthy phonic sessions, structured 'writing' tasks and some inappropriate adult-directed focused tasks. This behaviour should be seen as a message from the children – 'I don't find this engaging. This is not how I want to learn. Find a better way to support me!'

Unfortunately, in most schools, the blame is put on the children: 'They can't behave; they never push themselves; they can't concentrate; they have ADHD; they are lazy' etc. - the list is endless. I believe that if children are not engaged, then it is usually the fault of the school and it is the school that needs to change – not the children!

With this in mind, it is vital to be able to spot when children are engaged and when they are not, in order to be reflective of the practice on offer and in order to be able to evaluate any changes that are made. We use a scale devised by Professor Ferre Laevers which grades 'levels of involvement'.

The scale has five levels (see Appendix A). Level 5 is high level involvement and is characterised by the child showing continuous and intense activity with concentration, creativity, energy and persistence. Deep level learning, with many parts of the brain 'lit up', is known to occur when children operate at this level of involvement.

In contrast, low level involvement (Level 1) is characterised by activity that is simple, stereotypic, repetitive and passive, with little or no challenge and with the child appearing absent and displaying no energy. When children are operating at this level, there is very little brain activity and minimal learning.

These five levels of involvement can be used to assess individuals, groups or a whole class. Ferre Laevers also has a scale for the assessment of 'emotional well-being' but experience has shown that the two scales are very closely connected. For example, a child who is consistently displaying low level involvement, in spite of an outstanding environment and excellent practitioners, is very likely to have some emotional problem – perhaps related to an issue at home. However, the assessment of the level of involvement is the first step in assessing an individual or a setting.

Anyone who visits Carterhatch comments on how calm and purposeful the children are. They are actually assessing the levels of involvement, the amount of brain activity and

the amount of progress that is happening. They can see that the children are not stressed and nor are the staff. (Stress causes areas of the brain to shut down and therefore development is hindered.) The children are displaying high levels of involvement and so are the staff – indicating that dramatic progress is happening. I will endeavour, through this book, to explain how this can be achieved.

Organisation of the book

There are 11 chapters in the book – one for each month of the year that the school is open. Most chapters are divided into three sections. The first section looks at general, organisational, practical or theoretical issues – such as timetables, data, adult roles, transition, etc. These may be related to the particular month in which they appear or they may be ongoing issues. The second section is devoted to the description of various aspects of the physical environment. In order to meet the needs, stage of development and interests of each child, the provision and resources are crucially important. This is why a large proportion of the book is devoted to this subject. The third section is a diary of some events from that particular month – illustrating the teaching and learning that is happening constantly. This includes the interactions between the staff and the children and between groups of children, as well as examples of the independent learning that occurs.

It is an amazing achievement to have 90 Year One children directing their own play and all deeply involved and learning for the majority of every day that they are in school. This has taken careful organisation of the environment, development of a 'planning in the moment' system to ensure curriculum coverage by every child, and staff training to be certain that teachable moments are spotted and exploited in an appropriate way. Of course, none of this would be possible without the support of the leadership team in the school, but the leap of faith has yielded fantastic results and so the journey can continue. There is a vast amount of information that needs to be included in this book and it is all important. Each piece of information forms part of the whole picture and although you can dip in and out of each chapter, I hope you will read the whole book to ensure that you understand the complete rationale.

Theory into practice

I have been working in education for nearly 30 years – initially with adults and for the last 27 years in primary education. I have studied the theory of education and read research from around the world. However, in this book, I will be explaining how my years of experience, combined with mountains of reading, have led to a way of working that, finally, feels right for the children – it shows how the theory has been put into practice. I have lived through numerous government initiatives and statutory changes – many of which have been revoked once they have been shown to be misguided. Maybe the teachers should be asked their opinion before new ideas are introduced. Young children are still young children and it is the staff who work with them on a daily basis who know what they need; yet they are rarely, if ever, consulted. Even if teachers are consulted – their view is ignored if it does not fit with the government's agenda (testing, league tables, phonics screening, performance-related pay, etc.) As a result, many teachers are suffering from mental health problems, others are leaving the profession completely and numerous head teacher posts remain vacant. The incessant focus on data, targets and unrealistic expectations means that it is very difficult to take risks in a school. Everyone is 'playing it safe' – making sure the data is 'good' so that Ofsted cannot put the school into special measures, forcing head teachers to end their careers. However, in this fear-driven education system, it is the children who are suffering. The pressure on head teachers is forced down onto the teachers and in turn onto the children – with a curriculum narrowed to virtually nothing but literacy and numeracy and a formalisation of learning at a younger and younger age. We are the only country in the world which educates children in this way. There is a vast mountain of evidence to show how ineffective it is to force young children to learn in a

formal, adult-led way and yet that is what is happening to our youngest children. For the past ten years, I have been refusing to succumb to this fear and have been fortunate to work in schools where the head teachers have been brave and innovative, willing to take risks, to have faith in the evidence and to hold on to the belief that **children do want to learn**. We don't have to 'force' children to learn, we just have to find ways to teach them that are engaging, active and appropriate. The results have been truly inspiring – proving that, without formalisation, without extreme 'control', without fear, the children do thrive, they do learn and they want to go on learning! In recent months, I have felt more optimistic that teachers are willing to make a stand for what is right for the children. The more teachers that do this, the stronger the profession will become. The results will mean that we can go on working in a more developmentally appropriate way. Teachers need to support each other in resisting inappropriate initiatives and also in trialling new ways of working. Hopefully this book will inspire a few more teachers to try a new way of working – be brave, take a risk, cause a bit of a stir, **do what is right for the children**.

1 September

A unique month, a unique chapter

TO DO LIST

- Attend staff training.
- Prepare the class environment – indoors and outside.
- Prepare coat peg, self-register and an individual folder for each child.
- Welcome and support children and their families.
- Focus on PSE to ensure children are happy and expectations of behaviour are clear.
- Start first cycle of focus children.
- Start first cycle of parent meetings.
- Begin to record the learning and development of group activities.

Organisation

September is a critical month for any year group in school. It is the month in which expectations, routines and boundaries are established and consistently applied. Within these firm and clear guidelines, the children can then relax. It is only in this relaxed state that children can become deeply involved in their learning. They do not have to worry about what is going to happen, or what mood the adults are going to be in, or whether the resources they need are going to be available. They know what to expect, they know how to behave, they know the adults are going to keep them safe, they know they are valued and liked. In this state, they are 'safe' (emotionally and physically) to relax and to take risks – i.e. to try something new, a new experience, a new challenge, some new learning. As critical as it is, we need the transition period to be as quick and seamless as possible so that the children settle immediately, ensuring that no learning time is missed. This requires meticulous planning and preparation. Much of this work was started in the Summer Term and will be described in later chapters of this book. Here I will set out the work we do in September and how the children are inducted into their new year.

This chapter is organised a little differently to other chapters with a brief explanation of induction and the timetable, followed by an overview of the principles for an enabling environment, a look at behaviour management and then conflict resolution. The diary section gives just a hint at the vast amount of learning that took place in just the first few weeks of the year.

Day one

It is usually the case that nearly all the children joining Year One were in the same school for their Reception year and that was the case at Carterhatch in September 2015. Therefore we knew the children and their families and the children knew the staff and the environment. On the first morning, the staff that had been in Reception were at the gate to welcome the children and to take them into their new classes. The parents were encouraged to say goodbye at the gate. All but three of the children were absolutely confident to do this; they were delighted to see their friends and their old teachers, excited about going into their new class and happy to wave goodbye to their parents. A few children needed a parent to support them and this was accepted too. As with many schools, the logistics are difficult and it is just not possible to have 90 children, their parents and often their siblings too, all coming into the classrooms. Because we knew the children so well, we were confident that they would be happy with this system and indeed they were – within ten minutes of arriving, they were all engaged in their play and the parents had said goodbye.

Timetable

Our aim with the timetable in Year One is to maximise the length of periods during which the children are in control of their learning – i.e. the amount of time they are 'playing'. Therefore we have opted not to have morning or afternoon breaks, the children are not going to assembly, they do not leave the class for music, ICT or any other subject. In the first half term, they are also getting all their physical education within the class and garden environment, but PE lessons will be introduced after the first half term. The short adult-led inputs are either at the start or end of sessions, again to avoid interruptions. So the timetable for the first two weeks is very simple:

8.50 – 12.00	12.00 – 12.15	1.25 – 3.00	3.00 – 3.15
Self-register, Free-flow play Tidy up	Whole-class group time	Free-flow play Tidy up	Whole-class group time

(Self-registration involves the children ticking their name on a list. The adults also complete an electronic official register.) Lunch is 12.15 – 1.25.

Thus in the first two weeks the children have over four hours of free-flow play. During this time the children are deeply involved – purposeful, independent, confident, creative, energetic, enthusiastic, risk-taking, operating at their limits, co-operating, investigating, discovering, communicating – in other words – THEY ARE LEARNING! These 90 children were learning like this in their Reception year and made outstanding progress. We know them very well and we know that they thrive with this autonomous style of learning and we therefore want it to continue in Year One. In the diary section below, you can read about some of the amazing learning that happened in these first few weeks and hopefully any doubts about the value of 'play' will be dispelled.

In the second half of September, we gradually introduced three short adult-led sessions. Therefore by the end of September the daily timetable became:

8.50 – 9.20	9.20 – 11.40	11.40 - 12.00	12.00 – 12.15	1.25 – 1.40	1.40 – 3.00	3.00 – 3.15
Self-register Group reading	Free-flow play Tidy up	Maths input in groups	Whole-class group time	Phonics	Free-flow play Tidy up	Whole-class group time

The children still have over three hours of free-flow play, during which they can apply the skills and knowledge that they have gained in the reading, phonics and maths sessions. However, how and for what purpose they apply these will be unique to each child. In this way they are able to maintain their autonomy and can pursue their own interests as the diary sections will illustrate. No two children will have the same experience – their journey will be uniquely suited to them as individuals.

The adult-led sessions are pre-planned according to the assessments and information that we have for the children in Year One. The vast majority of this information was obtained from assessments carried out by the Reception teachers and, where necessary, adjusted according to observations made in the early part of Year One. The school has opted to follow a reading and maths programme in which children are in small groups with an adult each day. They also follow letters and sounds for the phonic work and these sessions are delivered by the Year One staff. For the purposes of this book, I am not going to detail the work in these sessions. There are vast amounts of materials available to support the teaching of such sessions and each school needs to find a programme that they wish to deliver. As with everything else that we do, we use 'Levels of Involvement' to assess whether the sessions are of value. Remember, if children are not showing good levels of involvement, then they are not learning. We will continually monitor the value of these sessions and adjust their length or content accordingly. It is critical to remember that phonics, reading and maths are not an end in themselves. They are a means to an end. We need to give the children these skills in order that they can learn about other things. The phonics screening test (that is currently carried out in Year One) has been one of the most damaging, in terms

These boys have chosen to write about their football match. They have collected their folders (see November chapter) to write in. It is also interesting to note that not one of them is sitting on a chair – even though the chairs are available.

of its effect on the curriculum in Year One. The emphasis on phonics has been dramatically and tragically exaggerated in many schools and the curriculum has been narrowed and simplified to the detriment of the children in Year One. We need to remember that if children (or adults!) are fascinated by a subject, then they will persevere, struggle and focus in order to learn. This will almost always involve aspects of language, literacy and maths. However, literacy and maths in isolation from anything interesting will not hold their attention, they will not persevere, struggle or focus and therefore the learning is much, much harder. Therefore the main content of this book will focus on the periods of the day when the children are applying these skills in their play. This is an area that has been neglected in educational materials and yet it is the most important part of the day for the children – the time when they are doing what interests them, when they are deeply involved and therefore when they are learning the most. These 'free-flow' sessions are not pre-planned – the adults observe and respond '**in the moment**' as described in more detail in the next chapter.

Setting up the environment

An enabling environment

It is a hugely complex task to organise the highest quality free-flow play in which 90 children can be engaged. It is rather like a jigsaw puzzle with many components and all are essential. The environment is one piece of the jigsaw – a perfect environment without all the other components will not support outstanding play. However, a class without an outstanding environment will not deliver outstanding play either. It is a very important piece of the picture and that is why it is given such prominence in this book. If the environment is perfect, all children can be fully engaged in purposeful play of their own choice and interest. I would also stress that the outdoor area is essential in supporting learning in Year One. These children are just five years old – they do not want to be sitting down indoors all day. Some of them never want to be sitting down and some never want to be indoors. Many children are more relaxed, happier and more engaged moving about and/or outdoors. Therefore, without a superb outdoor environment, we are not meeting the needs of many children. Equally, it is no good having an outdoor area, if it is not given the love and attention that the indoors is given. The outdoor areas are actually harder to maintain as the wind and rain batter the resources and the cleaners do not usually have it on their rota to clean. The staff team need to be fully committed to this way of working, they need to understand and witness the superb learning that can happen outdoors. Only then will they put in the effort necessary to maintain the outdoor area and go on to celebrate the results. The Year One staff at Carterhatch spent many days working on the outdoor area in the summer holidays and they continue to work incredibly hard, reviewing and maintaining the environment for the children.

In the remaining chapters of the book, various areas of the class and garden are described in detail. However, here I will outline the general principles which have been applied in the planning and organisation of the environment. Although various aspects of the environment are described in each chapter, the whole environment is set up and stocked before the children start in September. This is essential so that the children can be trained in how to use the various areas from day one. As in our nursery and Reception classes, we have a **workshop** setup both indoors and outside. This means that in all areas, the resources are available and accessible to the children at all times, but nothing is set out. So, therefore, **the tables are clear at the start of the day**, the sand and water are free of equipment (but the resources are available next to these areas), the wood is on the shelf near the workbenches, with the tools to hand, the blocks are in their usual position at the edge of the area, etc.

When a class is organised in this way, **the children are in control of their learning**. They are able to select the area in which to play, the resources to use in that area and what to do with them. Obviously their choices are limited by the areas and resources available and it is therefore crucial to have appropriate areas with varied, high-quality, open-ended resources. Details of resources in various areas will be covered in each chapter. It is also vital that the areas are well stocked, tidy, clearly labelled (with picture and word) or shadowed and arranged to allow optimum access. Each cohort of children will be different and their interests and curiosities will change over the period of the year. We constantly review and reflect on the environment to see which areas are proving productive and which need altering. For example, early in the term we realised that the children were not using the outdoor reading area. The staff moved this to one of the high platforms, along with some cushions, and the area immediately became more appealing and was used more often.

Similarly, the resources are assessed and reviewed constantly with changes made as necessary. When developing a workshop environment in Year One, it is essential that it will be challenging for the children. Some resources will be the same as nursery or Reception – for example pencils, paper, scissors, etc. can be used in different ways by children of all ages. Similarly, the woodwork area is used differently, even though it is essentially the same as that in the nursery. However, other resources need careful

The model that can be seen in this picture has taken over half an hour to build. This level of sophisticated play will not happen if the timetable does not allow for long periods of uninterrupted play.

consideration. For example, trikes would not challenge most Reception children, let alone Year One children and so would not be included. Equally, Duplo is appealing to children in nursery, but smaller, more intricate construction equipment is needed to engage children in Year One.

Because the children select and access resources themselves, they know where they are from and they know where to put them back when they have finished using them, or at the end of the session. Shadowing resources is used to aid this process – for example, as seen here with the indoor blocks. The 'shadows' are cut from coloured card or paper and glued to the shelf. Once the whole shelf is covered in 'sticky back' plastic, the shadowing will remain in place for several years – a task worth doing! This is very time-consuming but, once complete, the unit will stay tidy and the resources are seen to be valued and cared for.

Outdoors, it takes only five minutes to set up the garden. This is because as many resources as possible are left in position and if they are likely to be damaged by rain, then they are covered with tarpaulins, secured at night with elasticated rope. A video of the garden being set up can be seen at www.youtube.com/watch?v=dSlFzBezfig

This is a plan of the outdoor area:

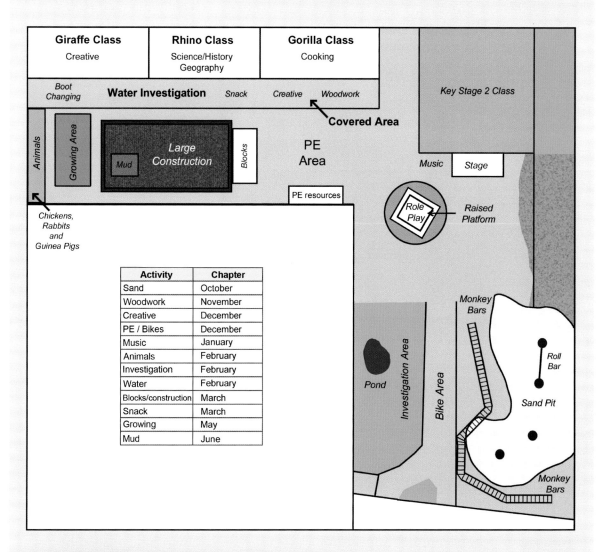

Activity	Chapter
Sand	October
Woodwork	November
Creative	December
PE / Bikes	December
Music	January
Animals	February
Investigation	February
Water	February
Blocks/construction	March
Snack	March
Growing	May
Mud	June

Indoors, it takes a short time to set up as well. Staff spend the period before school re-stocking and checking resources. The pictures opposite and below show two views of one classroom. The tables were clear at the start of the session – the resources in use have been put on the tables by the children. Staff do not spend time setting resources out on the tables. Another point to note is that there are not too many tables. Young children often prefer to be on the floor or at very low tables. Again the situation is reviewed throughout the year (using levels of involvement) and if we feel it is necessary, then more tables will be brought out of storage and into the classrooms.

It is interesting to note how many boys are indoors in the Year One classrooms. This is because indoors is equally as engaging as outdoors. It is not viewed as the area where 'work' is done. All areas – indoors and outside – are for 'playing' and the learning therefore happens in all areas too.

Organisation

As mentioned, the environment needs to be ready before the children start back in September. Although staff cannot be directed to work in the holidays, I don't know of any teacher who does not go in to get their classroom ready – for example shadowing, labelling resources, preparing coat pegs, organising folders, painting outdoor units if necessary, etc. The work done on these days means that when the children arrive, the environment is ready and as good as it can possibly be. In some cases, your senior leaders might give you an inset day on which you can work as a team to develop your outdoor area. I always have an ongoing wishlist and if ever we have inset time, then some things on that list can be crossed off. If you plan to approach your senior managers to ask for this valuable time, then you need to be sure to have an action plan prepared. Be clear about how the time will be used and how the work will benefit the children. Make sure you are aware of cost implications as well. Many tasks just require time, such as digging over some soil to create a mini-beast area or re-organising the layout of the class. Other tasks require minimal expense: covering units with tarpaulins or sorting plastic resources into shopping baskets. More expensive items will probably require a written bid to have been presented the summer before. Start your wish list and add to it as you read through this book, then prioritise and calculate some costs. The more organised and thoughtful you appear, the more likely you are to get agreement from your managers.

Behaviour management

If you get your provision right, then every child will be engaged in something that is meaningful and fascinating to them. In that situation, why would there be any behaviour issues? There would not and indeed that is what we have found. We don't need 'golden time' or stickers or behaviour charts or consequence charts, etc. Children who are deeply involved are too busy learning to cause any problems. Visitors always comment on how calm the children are and it is purely because they are engaged. Of course there are a few essential 'rules' and these are consistently, firmly and calmly applied.

- Indoors we walk and we use quiet voices.
- We use our words to sort out arguments.
- When we have finished playing in an area, we tidy it up before moving away.
- When climbing, no one touches anyone else.

As explained the vast majority of the children have come through nursery and Reception – they know these 'rules' and they accept them. For any new children and a few others, the teaching in the first few weeks (and sometimes longer) is the establishment of these boundaries and expectations. Occasional tantrums will occur and we are aware that some children are able to get exactly what they want at home by using such tantrums and other strategies. In school, we have to be careful to show that some things are non-negotiable, regardless of how angry it makes the child. For example, a boy who wanted to leave all the blocks on the floor found it very difficult to accept that this was not going to happen. In such cases, we need to be calm and clear in our response – it is not a time for negotiation. 'When you have put the blocks away, then you can go outside.' Once all children are clear about the expectations, then a 'zero tolerance' approach is established – ensuring clear, consistent messages are given. Having been a foster carer for ten years, I have learnt just how often some children will test the boundaries. Each time that the boundaries are re-established, the child will feel more and more secure (even though the staff might feel more and more exasperated!) A 'time-out' spot is used quickly and consistently, giving the child as little attention as possible. The message they are getting is that 'in school, this is the rule and it will always be the rule'. Although this may appear harsh, it is the quickest

Scenes such as the one seen in this photo are not possible if a room is crammed full of tables and chairs. Young children are very comfortable working on the floor and, if they are not in a sitting position all day, it is also good for their posture and their spine.

and kindest way to help the children understand that school is a predictable, safe, place in which they can relax and play and that the chaos or inconsistency, that some of them may experience at home, will not happen in school.

Conflict resolution

As mentioned, one of our rules is 'We use our words to sort out arguments' and for most of the children in Year One, this is automatic since they have been getting the same message for the two previous years. However, for the few new children, this skill needs to be taught. I will explain a little more about this for readers who are new to this way of working. If this teaching is successful, then the children will be independent in their dealings with each other. This means that staff are not spending lengthy periods sorting out arguments amongst the children. For example, if Mira snatches a toy from Ali, an adult will join the pair, give the toy back to Ali and then speak to Mira saying, 'If you want that toy, you need to ask Ali – so speak to her and say "Can I have that toy please?".' The adult will also then speak to Ali and say 'You don't have to give her the toy – you can say "No, I am using it" or "You can have it in a minute".' The adult will then encourage the pair to talk like this and resolve the dispute. If a child is upset because another child has shouted at them, the adult will again model a response and encourage the child to use it saying, for example, 'Don't shout at me. I don't like it.' It is not very helpful to say to children 'you need to share' or 'play nicely' as they don't know what that means. They need specific language such as 'You have it for three minutes and then I will have it for three minutes' (using a timer perhaps) or 'You have all four trains and I am sad because I have none. Can you give me some?'. If Tom is crying, an adult will ask 'what has happened?'. This is far easier for Tom to answer than 'Why are you crying?'. If they are crying because Amir has done something, then the adult will bring Amir over and encourage Tom to talk **to** Amir and **look at** Amir. He might need the language modelled but it is important that he speaks to Amir himself saying, for example, 'You hurt me when you ran past and you didn't stop to see if I was OK.' Amir must then be encouraged to respond – talking to and looking at Tom.

He might say, 'Oh I didn't realise I hurt you – sorry!'. If the children can come up with solutions for themselves, they will be more likely to find a solution the next time without calling on an adult. This level of independence is so valuable and frees the adults up to teach other things. In Year One, where adult numbers are fewer than in nursery or Reception, this independence is even more essential.

Diary extracts: examples of development and learning

WHAT TO LOOK OUT FOR

- The children settle quickly and are familiar with the staff and the setting.
- Resources are engaging the children.
- Resources are accessed easily and independently.
- Children explore all areas, take risks and try new experiences.
- Children follow the class routines and expectations.
- Children manage conflicts and negotiations independently.
- Most children demonstrate high levels of involvement for sustained periods.

In this diary section, I am going to look at some events that centre around individual children, demonstrating how broad the curriculum coverage can be, from some very simple starting points. I will also look at some things that involved groups of children – again covering broad sections of the curriculum – but, more importantly, being very memorable events for the children; memories that they will have for the rest of their lives. Children remember things from Year One in a more conscious way than they do from the early years.

Cakes

Efsun was in the large outdoor sand area. She found a circular cake tin and used it to make a 'sand cake'. She went on to add pine cones around the edge, but could not find enough to go all the way round. Jacqui suggested she spread the pine cones out but she was not satisfied with the gaps and so used conkers to fill in the spaces.

Sample learning journeys (see October chapter for explanation)

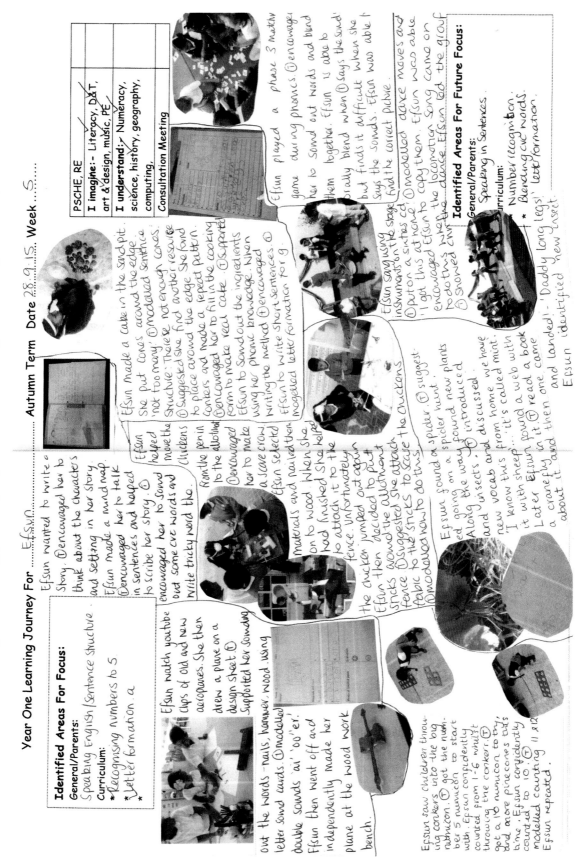

Year One Learning Journey For ....Efsun....   Autumn Term   Date 28.9.15. Week ...5...

Identified Areas For Focus:
General/Parents:
Speaking English/Sentence Structure.
Curriculum:
* Recognising numbers to 5
* Letter formation a
*

PSCHE, RE	
I imagine:- Literacy, D&T, art & design, music, PE	
I understand:- Numeracy, science, history, geography, computing.	
Consultation Meeting	

Efsun wanted to write a story. ⓣ encouraged her to think about the character's and setting in her story. Efsun made a mind map. ⓣ encouraged her to talk in sentences and helped to scribe her story. ⓣ encouraged her to sound out some cvc words and write tricky word the.

Efsun made a cake in the sandpit. She put cones around the edge ⓣ modelled sentence 'not too many'/'not enough cones.' ⓣ Suggested she find another resource to place around the edge. She found conkers and made a repeat pattern. ⓣ encouraged her to fill in the cooking form to make real cake. ⓣ supported Efsun to sound out the ingredients using her phonic knowledge. When writing the method ⓣ encouraged Efsun to write short sentences. ⓣ modelled letter formation for g.

Efsun played a phase 3 match game during phonics ⓣ encouraged her to sound out words and blend them together. Efsun is able to orally blend when ⓣ says the sound but finds it difficult when she says the sounds. Efsun was able to say the sounds. Efsun was able to had the correct picture.

Efsun sang using instruments on the stage ⓣ put this at home. ⓣ modelled dance moves and encouraged Efsun to copy them. Efsun was able to the locomotion song came on the dance Efsun led the group to do this. ⓣ showed cvc

Identified Areas For Future Focus:
General/Parents:
Speaking in Sentences.
Curriculum:
* Number recognition
* Blending cvc words
* Letter formation

Efsun watch youtube clips of old and new aeroplanes. She then drew a plane on a design sheet ⓣ supported her sounding out the words - nails, hammer, wood. Using letter sound cards. ⓣ modelled double sounds 'ai' 'oo' 'er'. Efsun then went off and independently made her plane at the wood work bench.

Efsun helped move the chickens. From the pen/to the allotment ⓣ encouraged how to make a scare crow. Efsun selected materials and narrated when she on to wood. When she had finished she helped to attach it to the fence. Unfortunately the chicken jumped out again Efsun then decided to put wood/the allotment fence ⓣ suggested she attach fabric to the sticks to scare the chickens to do this. ⓣ modelled how to do this.

Efsun found a spider. ⓣ suggest ed going the way found new plants Along and insects. ⓣ introduced new vocab and discussed we have from home it's called mint. "I know sheep" ... "it's called with it with sheep" Efsun found a web with Later Efsun read a book a cranefly in it. ⓣ read a book a cranefly and then one came and landed. "Daddy long legs" Efsun identified new insect.

Efsun saw children throwing conkers into the big numicon. ⓣ got the number 5 numicon to start with. Efsun confidently counted from 1-6 whilst throwing the conkers. ⓣ got a 10 numicon to try and more piececones this time. Efsun confidently counted to 10. ⓣ modelled counting 11 x12 Efsun repeated.

Identified Areas For Focus:

General/Parents:
develop interest in superheroes.

Curriculum:
* counting and recognising n° to 10.
* practise phase 2 sounds + blending.
* managing his feelings and resolving problems with friends.

M wanted to make a dog mask. T encouraged him to gather resources, and iPad. T needed support with other sounds. M chose the dog picture 'needs to have a blue hat'. and drew it. M showed very good attention and was engrossed for 5+ mins drawing it. m "their are the ears, the hat" T encouraged M to find a darker colour for the eyes. M showed good independence in cutting out eye holes and attaching a strap to his mask. "voila" He said when finished.
"woof, woof"

M found a spider "RACHEL look SPIDER!" M was very interested. T encouraged M to find a book on spiders- he brought one. T modelled using the contents page to model find the info he wanted. M looked through the pages commenting on what they were marking T what they were reading T with their names and read them out.

M had 5p in his bum bag. "I want to buy paper" he said. T encouraged M to check the price. T supported M to read "1p". T explained this is "1pence". "How much?" M said "1 pence". He took a 1p from his bag and put it in the till. Shortly after M wanted more paper. T encouraged him to think about spending his money throughout the day rather than all at once. M spend the rest of the money independently.

T suggested M tell her a story about his dog. "yes!" M encouraged T supported M to choose 4 characters M decided which friends would be the characters in his play. T scribed M's story. m tried writing the end.

Muhammet was stood at the monkey bars and was struggling to reach. "I'm scared." T encouraged him to find a starting place with a higher mound so he could reach. He managed to hang from it and was very pleased! T encouraged M to watch another child model moving forwards. M went comfortable along this yet. M returned to the smaller mound + pushed himself to jump- he reached it!

M was playing with a magnet with a friend. T modelled language "magnet" M noticed it didn't stick to everything. T encouraged him to test the magnet on different material. M identified metal and wood. T encouraged M to predict whether the magnet would stick to a tree. "No!" he said. T asked "why?" m wasn't sure how to explain this. M tested the magnet on the tree. T explained about the wood and tree being the same material.

"PSCHE, RE"

I imagine:-	Literacy, D&T, art & design, music, PE
I understand:-	Numeracy, science, history, geography, computing.
Consultation Meeting	

Muhammet build with lego along side Lee. he puts his building next to Lee "mine big" T encourage him to use a tape measure to check to see which is the longest. Muhammet was unsure what a tape measure was T shows him and model how to use it. T model his building T use what numbers on the end "don't know" T model counting using his finger from 0-10. Muhammet repeats T explains that the last number is the total measurement. 10 inch Muhammet repeat.

M was making cake with friends. T encouraged M to help his friends. When weighing the ingredients T "which side is heavy now M" M points in the right direction. T praise M. T encourage M to take turns with his friend. M "it's to hard to stir" T "I have added a little milk, how is it now" M "easy to mix" T explaining why that is. M "when can I make my cake. T "after it is cooked" T

Identified Areas For Future Focus:

General/Parents:

Curriculum:
* Counting + recognising number to 20
* Phase 2 sounds- initial sounds and blending.

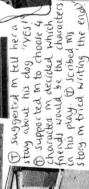

She then said that she would like to use this mould to make a real cake and set about completing the design sheet. (See Appendix B.)

 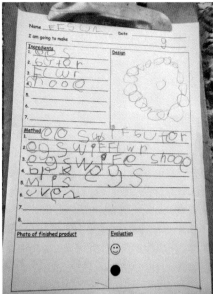

Later in the day, Efsun made her cake with a group of friends. (They did this without adult support – using the balance method that they had learnt in Reception.) Efsun decorated the cake with chocolate buttons to replicate the pine cones and conkers.

In the October chapter, I will explain about our system of focus children, and Efsun was one of the focus children on this day. When back-tracking to the national curriculum, the coverage from this one day is broad and deep, including personal and social skills (which are not given much emphasis in the national curriculum in Year One!), science (materials, changing states, seeds – conkers), communication and language (discussions, questions, planning), literacy (writing, reading lists and instructions), maths (shape, pattern, weight, time), design and technology (plan, do, review). Efsun probably went home and said 'I played in the sand and I had cake!' . . . which indeed she did, but along the way, the learning was substantial, meaningful and fun!

The solar system

Lee used the iPad to look at plane designs and then used Lego to make an aeroplane and a spiderman. He started chatting about where they would fly and Rachel suggested that he drew a map to show where they were going. He included the earth, moon and sun on his map as well as 'meteorites' and 'stars'. He asked how many planets there were and Rachel encouraged him to think how he could find out. He looked on the iPad and discovered lots of information about the 'solar system'. Lee didn't know that men had been to the moon and so looked this up on the iPad. He said 'It's in black and white so it was a long time ago!'. He noticed the flag and knew that it was from 'America'. Later he drew a picture of an astronaut and rocket, created a story map including characters, setting and events, and then dictated the story from his plan. Rachel and Lee shared the writing for the story and later the story was read aloud while a group acted it out (with clear directions from Lee). (See November chapter for an explanation of story scribing.)

Once again, what started out as a simple activity led to broad curriculum coverage, new knowledge being acquired and challenges overcome. Lee started the day building with Lego, but by the end of the day he had covered communication and language, literacy, design and technology, science, ICT, geography and history! He was deeply involved all day, new synapses formed, self-esteem was boosted and he had great fun too!

Mending mum's toy

The focus children are invited to bring in a few items from home to show to the class. Kayra brought in an old toy that used to belong to her mum when she was a child. Kayra took great pride in showing her things to the class and talking about each of them in turn. When it came to the toy, she explained that it was so old that it had lost one of its eyes. Ruth suggested that Kayra would be able to mend the toy since we have sewing equipment available. Kayra set about doing this and was delighted with the result.

Through this simple chain of events, Kayra covered numerous areas of the curriculum – communication and language, history, design and technology and physical development. She also made a book about 'Topsy' (see the photo above) and therefore developed her literacy skills too.

Bingo

Several children discovered the 'bingo' game on the iPads. It has a simple sum at the top of the screen and the answer appears in one of the boxes on the main part of the screen. The children used various strategies to calculate the answers – some using mental recall, some using Numicon, some using their fingers. An adult introduced a number line as another option – explaining how to mark the 'jumps' up the line to find the answer. Several children started using this method and explaining it to their friends.

A new pond

Several children were talking about the 'pond' that they had in nursery and Jacqui suggested that they could possibly have a pond in Year One too. They started to research how to make a pond and found that an old tractor tyre could be turned into a pond. Two children then wrote to the health and safety officer for the school to check where they could place the pond (this involved drawing a plan of the area as well) and they also wrote to my husband to ask him to cut off the rim of the tractor tyre.

 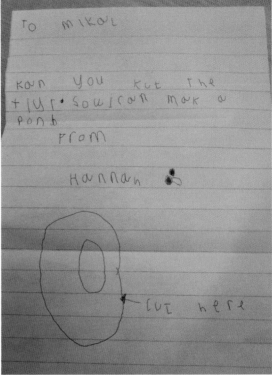

I got involved showing the children how to check that the pond would be level, then the pond was put in place and filled with water and plants. Michael and some other children became interested in the markings on the containers that they were using to transport the water and discussions led to an introduction to volume measurements of 1,000ml, etc.

Crocodiles

The interest in the possible creatures in the pond led on to other discussions about animals that live in the water. Osuani wanted to find out where crocodiles live and worked with some friends drawing pictures and reading all about crocodiles. They discovered that a crocodile could be six metres long and an adult suggested they could use metre sticks to see how long this actually was. In the corridor, the metre sticks were put in a line and then the children decided to find out how many children would fit inside the crocodile – the answer was five!

Many practitioners panic if they have not written down exactly who has done which activity. They also panic if some children do not access a particular activity. Experience shows that children (and adults) will engage with, and remember, those things that interest them. There is a saying that 'a pig does not get fatter by being measured' and I think we would be wise to remember this. The most important factor is engagement. If all the children are engaged, then relax and trust that they are learning. The detail of each individual activity is not as important as the engagement.

Some of the activities that occurred during September were recorded by the staff on learning journeys and staff record sheets and this is described in more detail in the next chapter.

As September comes to an end, it is clear that the children are already making fantastic progress. This is evident in the deep levels of involvement that are seen in the majority of the children for the majority of the day – they are willing to take risks, they are relaxed and they are obviously enjoying themselves. This does not happen by accident – they understand the expectations of behaviour, they understand and adhere to the few, essential rules, the environment is meeting their needs and catering to their interests (meaning that in many instances they can learn independently, in co-operation with their peers and from each other) and the staff are interacting skilfully to ensure that as many possible learning opportunities are captured and developed. The year is off to a wonderful start.

2 | October

In this chapter, I will explain the weekly routines, including the system of 'focus children', 'in the moment planning' and record keeping. As stated, there are written forward plans for the three adult-led sessions each day (reading, maths and phonics). However, the free-flow sessions are not planned, there are no activities set out, no pre-decided learning objectives and no focused activities. The adults' role during these sessions is to 'teach' the children as they play. There are 90 children, three class teachers, three support assistants, one adult working as individual support for two children with additional needs and one extra learning support assistant who works across the whole year group. The three class teachers take their PPA time at different times and are covered by the extra support assistant. Thus there are usually seven available adults and 90 children in the Year One area. In the environment section of this chapter, I will describe the sand area outside and the cooking unit indoors. The diary, this month, looks at a couple of examples of learning from these two areas of the environment and also looks in detail at the sample learning journeys to clarify exactly how they are completed, as well as outlining the adult role more explicitly.

TO DO LIST

- Ensure staff are clear about their role.
- Continue to establish expectations and ground rules.
- Continue recording the learning and development of groups.
- Continue the first cycle of focus children.
- Continue the first cycle of parent meetings.
- Reflect on and amend the environment if necessary.
- Update individual folders.

Organisation

The weekly routine – focus children and parental involvement

On Friday each week we select the 'focus children' for the following week. This is ten per cent of the class – so in Year One, that is three children in each class, i.e. nine across the year group. Each child will be a focus child once per term. At the beginning of the year we tend to choose children who have settled quickly, show good levels of involvement and appear quite confident. There are many reasons for this: they will be able to cope with some close attention; they are confident enough for staff to give them some appropriate challenges; also their learning journey sheet (see details below) will be completed quite quickly – this is important at this early stage of the year, because the staff still have to work hard ensuring all children are adhering to the expectations and boundaries. Once the children have been selected, they are given a parent consultation sheet to take home (see Appendix C). We speak to the parents and explain that we would like them to fill in the sheet in as much detail as possible and to return the sheet on Monday along with (for the Autumn Term) some special items that the child would like to show to the class. To the left, is an example of a completed parent sheet.

The information provided by the parents is fascinating and we often find out about events that the child might never have revealed – visiting relatives, family events, new pets, etc. In the early years these 'focus children' also take home a camera, taking pictures at home over the weekend to share with the class the following week. In Year One, in the Autumn Term, we ask them to bring in items of significance from home and we encourage the child to talk to the class about the items as they are shown.

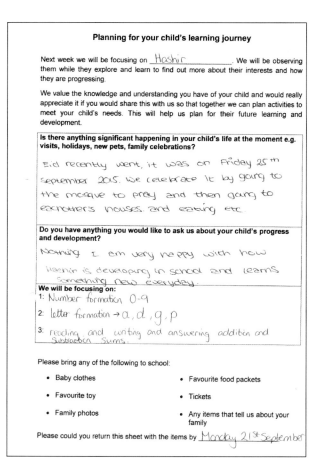

Planning for your child's learning journey

Next week we will be focusing on _Hashir_. We will be observing them while they explore and learn to find out more about their interests and how they are progressing.

We value the knowledge and understanding you have of your child and would really appreciate it if you would share this with us so that together we can plan activities to meet your child's needs. This will help us plan for their future learning and development.

Is there anything significant happening in your child's life at the moment e.g. visits, holidays, new pets, family celebrations?

Eid recently went, it was on Friday 25th September 2015. We celebrate it by going to the mosque to pray and then going to eachother's houses and eating etc

Do you have anything you would like to ask us about your child's progress and development?

Nothing I am very happy with how Hashir is developing in school and learns something new everyday.

We will be focusing on:
1: _Number formation 0-9_
2: _letter formation → a, d, g, p_
3: _reading and writing and answering addition and subtraction sums._

Please bring any of the following to school:

- Baby clothes
- Favourite toy
- Family photos
- Favourite food packets
- Tickets
- Any items that tell us about your family

Please could you return this sheet with the items by _Monday 21st September_

The focus children share some items from home. This is usually done at the end of the day.

Learning journey sheets

On Monday one A3 size learning journey sheet is put up on the planning board for each of the focus children. (See Appendix D.) These sheets are blank at the start of the week, except for the name, date and a couple of notes to remind staff about any particular areas that we wish to focus on with this child and anything that the parents have asked us about. You will find examples of completed learning journeys in several chapters of the book.

As mentioned, for a large portion of the day, we have 90 children initiating their own play and learning. To support these sessions, we have set up an enabling environment that is the best we can possibly have and we encourage the children to explore and learn by pursuing their own interests. The staff observe and interact with all the children in their pursuits – looking out for 'teachable moments' in which they can make a difference. They do not try to record all interactions as this would detract too much from the teaching time. However, they do record some of their interactions with the focus children on the learning journeys. The interactions that they choose to record are those where they have had an impact on the child and the child has made progress as a result. This process contains a moment in which the adult has to 'plan' what to do as a result of what they have observed. All adults who interact with a focus child contribute to the learning journeys.

In many settings, if 'free-flow' play happens at all, then observations are written down and ideas for 'next step activities' are planned and delivered at a later date. In these cases the next free-flow session is less free, with adults trying to carry out these activities. This is often quite stressful as the children are no longer interested and it also takes adults away from the crucial role of interacting with the children '**in the moment**'. We do not do any such forward planning – rather we remain 'in the moment' with the children and respond immediately. If a child is concentrating on using a drill at 2pm on Monday, that is the moment in which a skilful adult can interact with that child and 'teach' them how to use the drill effectively. The child is motivated and interested in that moment and therefore keen to learn. Such an interaction might appear on a learning journey as follows: ('T' indicates 'adult'.)

> Ryan was trying to drill but the wood kept moving. 'T' reminded Ryan about using the vice. 'T' modelled how to hold the drill firmly and turn the handle clockwise. Ryan watched carefully and then copied the technique correctly. He succeeded in drilling a small hole in the wood.

We highlight the 'teaching' in yellow and **it is vital that the entries on the learning journeys do contain an element of teaching**. Observations, without any 'plan' or 'teaching' are recorded but not included on the learning journeys – rather they are stored separately in the child's individual folder.

Another example might read:

> Baran was playing with the Bee-Bot. 'T' suggested he draw a map to show the way from a house to the shop. Baran drew a careful map. 'T' encouraged him to program the Bee-Bot to travel from the house to the shop and modelled how to input the instructions. After several attempts, Baran succeeded. 'T' gave praise for his perseverance.

Many entries at this early point in the year will refer to language development. Such entries are quite short and simple, but vitally important in terms of the 'teaching' and the progress that the child makes as a result. For example:

> Georgia says 'my want apple'. 'T' models '**I** want **an** apple'. Georgia repeats phrase correctly.

In all these examples, the children made progress in a very short space of time. Whenever anyone is observing free-flow play, I will try to be with them in order to point out the progress being made and the 'teaching' that enabled the progress to happen. I am often asked about 'next steps' and how these are noted/remembered. I point out that when working 'in the moment', the next steps are carried out immediately and therefore we do not need to record them anywhere else. I have visited many settings where they have written down literally hundreds of 'next steps' and the staff are stressed trying to remember them all and trying to find time to teach them!

The diagram on the next page shows the traditional teaching cycle that is recognised as best practice. The timescale for the duration of the cycle is where our 'in the moment' practice differs from the majority of settings. Each adult will complete the whole cycle hundreds of times each day (some of which are recorded) whereas in other settings the cycle is spread over a day or a week, with observations happening one day and the resulting activity happening the next day or the next week.

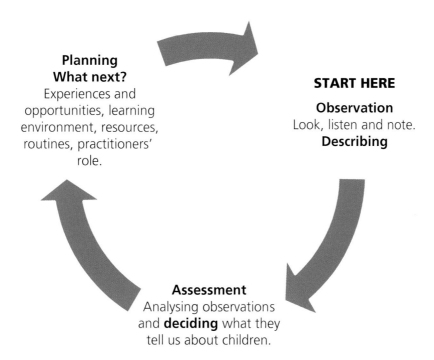

**Planning
What next?**
Experiences and opportunities, learning environment, resources, routines, practitioners' role.

START HERE

Observation
Look, listen and note.
Describing

Assessment
Analysing observations and **deciding** what they tell us about children.

Experience has shown that when this cycle is completed in a matter of moments, then the learning is powerful.

In September 2015, the common inspection framework included this definition of teaching in the early years section of the handbook. However, I believe it is a superb description of teaching for a child of any age.

> Teaching should not be taken to imply a 'top down' or formal way of working. It is a broad term which covers the many different ways in which adults help young children learn. It includes their interactions with children during planned and child-initiated play and activities: communicating and modelling language, showing, explaining, demonstrating, exploring ideas, encouraging, questioning, recalling, providing a narrative for what they are doing, facilitating and setting challenges.

These are exactly the sorts of things which we record on our learning journeys.

We often take a photo of the events and these are added to the learning journey as well. By the end of the week, the sheet is full of notes and photos – a unique record of that child's learning and development in that week. Further examples of completed sheets appear in several chapters of the book. Teachers who have tried this way of working report that, not only are they re-inspired and happy in their role, they have also got to know the children very well and as unique individuals. The teacher keeps a colour copy of each learning journey in their planning file, the parents get a copy and the original copy goes in the child's folder.

Parent meetings

In the week following their focus week, **we invite the parents of the focus children into school for a discussion about the week** and all that we have learnt about these children. We discuss any points that the parents have written on the consultation form and encourage them to add comments to their child's folder. Together we agree on possible areas for focus in future and how we can all support the children with these. Thus the teachers carry out three parent meetings each week, on a rolling cycle – far more meaningful, personal and informed than the traditional parent evenings when teachers sit for hours talking to each parent in turn.

Planning for the rest of the class

'What about the children who are not the focus children?'. This is a question I am asked over and over. The answer is simple. The other children carry on with their own learning journeys (even though they are not recorded in the same way). Sometimes they journey on their own, sometimes with a friend or a group and sometimes by joining an activity with one of the focus children. Also the adults are not totally absorbed with the focus children – this would be overwhelming for those children. The adults are often free to support other individuals or groups and they record such activities in their 'planning' file. Again, these activities are not pre-planned; rather they happen in response to observations and events. As with the individual children, staff will look out for activities or events that have captured the interest of a group. They will join the group to see if they can support, enhance or develop the activity in any way. Thus they are observing and assessing. Sometimes the group is operating independently and with deep level involvement (see Introduction) and any attempt to join the activity might actually disrupt it. In this situation the adult may observe for a while, possibly taking particular note of some children and then move away. However, on many occasions a skilful adult will spot a 'teachable moment'. They then decide what to do – this is **planning**. They might provide an extra resource, an idea, some vocabulary, some information, or they might model a skill or demonstrate how to use a piece of equipment – this is **teaching**.

  The teacher will keep a record of these events and back-track to the national curriculum to ensure coverage. Not all the children will access all the activities and we therefore track each child's coverage of the curriculum in their individual files (see November chapter for details). There are hundreds of examples of such events in the teachers' files, for example:

The children were trying to keep the chickens out of the vegetable patch but the chickens kept flapping and managing to get over the fence. 'T' explained the role of scarecrows on farms. The children looked at images of scarecrows on the internet and then made some in the woodwork area to attach to the fence.

There is a detailed discussion about woodwork in the November chapter, along with a 'benefit/risk assessment'. The extra resources – bottle tops, fabric, marker pens, etc. – are all available in the woodwork area so that the children can enhance their work as they wish.

Another example was:

> Children using pots and pans to catch the rain water from the roof. 'T' suggested they use the containers from the water area so that they could measure how much water they caught. The children fetched various containers and 'T' explained how to read the measurements. Several children began to read and use three digit numbers.

The children have access to the outdoor area at all times (unless there is a thunder storm). However, as this photo shows, some resources, such as the wooden blocks, are not available in wet weather as they would get ruined.

The photos on the following pages show some examples from a teacher's folder. The curriculum booklet is available to download at www.creativecascade.co.uk and is used by staff for each individual child.

With all this wonderful teaching, the children soon start to do things independently and when such moments are observed we refer to them as 'Wow!' moments – see November chapter for details. For example, after making his scarecrow, Kaan was heard explaining to another child about what it was for and how to make it. This was recorded in his file as evidence of his language development. Similarly, when it rained again later in the week, Abdi brought his container to an adult and said 'Look – I have 150 millilitres'. This was recorded as evidence of his maths development.

Numeracy

Measurement

	Emerging	Expected	Exceeding
✗ I can solve problems for length and height by telling which objects are longer or shorter/ taller or shorter.			
✗ I can solve problems for mass and weights by telling which objects are heavier or lighter.			
✗ I can solve problems for capacity and volume by telling if a container is empty, half full and if there is more in one container than another.			
✗ I can solve problems for time. I can tell if something is quicker or slower. I can tell if something happened earlier or later.			
I can measure weight or mass and write these measurements down.			
I can measure capacity or volume and write these measurements down.			
I can measure time in hours, seconds or minutes and write these measurements down.			
✗ I can tell how much different coins or notes are worth.			
✗ I can tell when things happened by using these words: before, after, next, first, today, yesterday, tomorrow, morning, afternoon, evening.			
I can talk about dates using the days of the week, weeks, months and years.			
I can tell what the time is in hours and half past the hour. I can draw these on a clock face.			
✗ I can measure and begin to record length/ height.			

A group of children were throwing hoops. ⊤ suggested measuring distance. The group moved to the 'alley' in the outdoor area near year 2. As the children were very excited to all start there hoops kept on knocking into each other, ⊤ asked them to stop and get a skipping rope to make a start line. ⊤ suggested 2 children going at a time. Children saw it worked better and waiti very patiently. Some children measured the distance of their hoops. One child held measuring tape for another child without prompt. ⊤ pointed to number on tape to show measurements. 'I got 30!'...'I got 70!'.

week 9 (9)

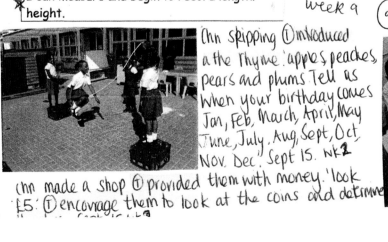

Chn skipping ⊤ introduced a the rhyme 'apples peaches, pears and plums Tell us when your birthday comes Jan, Feb, March, April, May June, July, Aug, Sept, Oct, Nov, Dec.' Sept 15. wk2

Chn made a shop ⊤ provided them with money. 'look £5' ⊤ encourage them to look at the coins and determ

chn making bracelets ①modelled how to measure their wrists. Reminding them to always start on zero. Sept 15 Wk 3.

Group of children were arguing about taking turns on the bikes (3 had been waiting with the timer). ⓣ encouraged them to get numicon. Children all got 1 numicon pieces. ⓣ - 'how will you know who's first, second and third? Children went and got 1, 2 & 3 between them.

Chn made pizzas ①encouraged them to write the ingredients and method down before they made the pizza and ask there friends which toppins they would like. Chn filled in this information on a bar chart and compared the findings - chicken won. Oct 15 Wk 6.

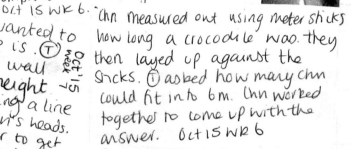

A group of children wanted to see how tall everyone is. ⓣ set up paper on the wall for them to measure height. Oct 15 week Children began drawing a line above different children's heads. ⓣ advised using a ruler to get x flat line. Children collected ifferent heights but ran out f time to measure with a ruler.

Chn measured out using meter sticks how long a crocodile was. they then layed up against the sticks. ⓣ asked how many chn could fit into 6m. Chn worked together to come up with the answer. Oct 15 Wk 6

Group making watches ⓣ encouraged group to look at a clock face and add numbers to their clocks. ⓣmodelled no. formation. ⓣexplained the positions of the hands to make o'clock. Oct 15 Wk 7.

A group of chn made guns and fired bullets. ⓣ introduced a game to measure how far the bullets had travelled. ①modelled vocab metres.

Jan 16. Wk 1

A group of chn gave each other CPR. (T) explained the dangers of doing that on someone breathing. The group then found books on the body and arranged the pieces of a magnetic skeleton. (T) gave chn labels and encouraged them to read them and place them next to the correct body part. (T) support when necessary. (T) then explained some of the labels and helped the chn to understand that they are senses. Sept 15 wk 3

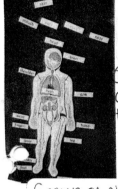

Group of children found a spider. They then found 2 others, one small + one very small. Children talked about them being babies.
(T) Asked them to look at them closely and see the differences. Talked about it being a different type of spider, like a different type of dog.
Sept 15 wk 3.

Group of children called me over to pond - 'a frog!' (T) 'It's nearly a frog but what is it now?'.. 'it's a tad - ' 'pole!'. Children talked about it being small and then getting bigger, then growing legs. (T) modelled language froglet.
Sept 15 wk 5.

Chn made nature pictures of things they have seen in the garden. Were able to recognise common animals. Sept 15 wks.

Group of chn made a zoo. All the animals were in together. (T) suggested making them separate pens and explained the difference between herbivores and carnivorous animals. Sept 15 wk 4.

Group made a farm. (T) discussed which animals live in farms and those that live in zoos. Chn changed model to a zoo and put animals in pens according to what they eat. Oct 15. wk 5.

Chn became interested in animals (T) introduced vocab herbivore, carnivore, omnivore and encouraged them to make a bar graph to compare how many of the animals they where researching fell into each category. Oct 15 Wk 6.

Chn used the ipad to find out facts on crocodiles. (T) encouraged them to write the facts down on a poster. Chn found out what they eat, where they live, how long they are. and that they are carnivours. Oct 15 Wk 6

A group of children saw their friend making a home for a woodlouse. Through discussion they found out what the insect was and what it liked, prompted by (T). Children helped friend and discovered other insects, - 'look a worm!' 'a beetle'. (T) showed children a picture and asked 'is this the same one?' in a minibeast book. - 'umm... yes!' (T) told them it was an earwig. Children found funny, 'errgh! earwig?!' week 9 (S)

A group of children were balancing on the window sill outside in different poses. (T) praised the (aj) shapes and silhouettes they were making, encouraging them to get some big paper to record. Children got role of paper and helped to stick up. (T) showed how you could trace round an arm and hand. Children took it in turns to trace round each other's bodies. As this was hard to do against the window, (T) suggested putting paper on floor. Children tried out different poses and traced whilst talking after about particular bits of the body - 'look at hexi's leg!' week 9 Nov

A group of children were excited about getting guineapigs and had a book on Mammals. (T) went through book with them. Children asked questions about names and habitats. The children were able to make comparisons between polar bears and brown bears as well. as knowing that one type of dolphin was different from another - 'He's got a big nose but he is still a dolphin'. Children carried on making simple deductions from pictures - 'he's eating blood but he's eating fish'. (T) prompted by asking questions throughout Nov Wk 9

Setting up the environment

Sand area outdoors

This sand area was built on a piece of land that had not been used for several years. It was adjacent to the Year One outdoor area and it was therefore a logical step to turn it into something useful.

This outdoor area is one of the most popular. Our sandpit is huge, but a large sandpit can easily be built from treated sleepers. The sleepers are relatively cheap to buy and can be placed directly onto a hard surface. Fixings are not essential as the sleepers are so heavy that small children cannot usually move them. Washed silver sand is ideal to fill the area and then resources need to be stored nearby. We have attached metal shopping baskets to the fence – ours are attached with cable ties, but if you have a wooden fence then the baskets can be hung on cup hooks. There is a photo and word above each basket to help with tidying up. These baskets are fantastic as they can be left out all the time – the resources are plastic or natural and the rain goes through the baskets. The baskets contain buckets, spades, vehicles, moulds, sieves and natural resources (shells, conkers, twigs, stones, bark, etc.). Close by is another unit with plates, cutlery, saucepans, etc. for the inevitable cooking that takes place, along with a small table and

chairs to promote role play. We have a second 'role play' area on a raised platform and have attached a pulley so that items can be hauled up and down. We have also placed two sets of giant Numicon on coat hooks (again, attached to the fence with cable ties).

Top tip – laminating

The labels above the baskets have been up for over a year. The secret to long-lasting labels is to ensure that the laminating sheet is much bigger than the picture – about three centimetres all round is good. Then, when you put the picture up, make sure that the holes (for cable ties) or staples (going into wood) go through the clear laminating sheet and not through the paper. If you pierce the paper, the rain will get in the first day that it rains. Staple (or hole punch) through the clear sheet and your labels will last all year and beyond.

The levels of involvement in this area are always high. Young children need opportunities to role play. When they do this, they are 'stepping into the role of another person', they are imagining what it is like to be another person. This is how they learn to empathise – a crucial life skill.

Most of the sandpits in school are covered with a tarpaulin at night – held in place with tyres placed on top. However, the Year One sandpit is too large and we therefore have to check it each morning, looking for animal footprints and other 'gifts' left

behind overnight. The sand outdoors is usually wet – either from the rain or from water transported to the area by the children. This allows for sandcastles, volcanoes, tunnels, rivers and mountains etc. to be built. We observe high levels of involvement in this area – children are fascinated by sand, its properties and its potential. When I visit other settings, I often advise practitioners to spend a day in the sandpit – observe the children carefully in their play and find out why they are so fascinated. Remember **children do not want to be bored** – if they are spending long periods in the sand, it is because it is deeply engaging for them. It is a teacher's job to find out what is going on in that brain when a child is so involved in their play in the sand.

Cooking units indoors

The classrooms at Carterhatch are not very large and we do not have a dedicated cooking room either. Therefore, we have created 'cooking units' which can be wheeled in and out of classrooms from the corridor where they are stored – or the items needed can be collected and taken into the classes. The photo opposite shows one of the units, and the second one contains further utensils, cookery books and some basic ingredients. Our children have come through a foundation stage in which cooking was a regular event. In Year One, their enthusiasm for cooking has not waned and tasty treats are regularly designed and prepared. In the early years, the children were encouraged to draw what they were going to make and, if appropriate, they would have dictated an ingredients list for an adult to scribe, and they would have contributed to this process as appropriate for that child. In Year One, we have prepared a 'design' sheet for the cooking area – see Appendix B. The completion of this sheet will continue to be a shared process if that is what is developmentally appropriate for the child. We will not cause a child anxiety by forcing them to write if they are developmentally not at that stage. Some children can form letters beautifully but do not have phonological awareness that is sophisticated enough to write at length. Other children have the phonological awareness but cannot hold a pencil firmly enough because, physically, they are not at that stage. Every child is unique – and we never forget that. They are all operating at their limit and we will support them to take the tiny jump in development that is appropriate at the time. The design sheet involves writing a title, a list and instructions – covering some of the vast literacy requirements of the national curriculum. The cookery books are a mixture of those that we have created ourselves (see Appendix E) and others that we have purchased. However, we encourage the children to create their own recipes and methods, perhaps using the books for initial ideas.

We use an online shopping order to keep stocked up with basic ingredients but if special items are needed, then shopping lists are written and, if possible, a group will go to the local shops or a note is written to an adult asking them to buy the items on their way home! (Letter writing? – Tick!) As with everything that we have on offer, the cooking is always available; the children know this and, therefore, there is not a mad rush to have a turn. The children know that if they don't get a chance to cook their creation today, there will always be another chance. As long as our environment is delivering high levels of involvement, then we do not change it. The cooking units will always be there, as there are always children keen to cook and huge learning potential to be tapped into.

Osuani has put a great deal of effort into this piece of writing. He knew that once the design sheet was complete, he would get to make his pancakes. I have never seen this level of commitment and care given to an exercise in a literacy book, when the child knows that the only outcome might be a sticker or a 'well done' from the teacher. A chance to cook and eat a real pancake is a far more powerful incentive to write.

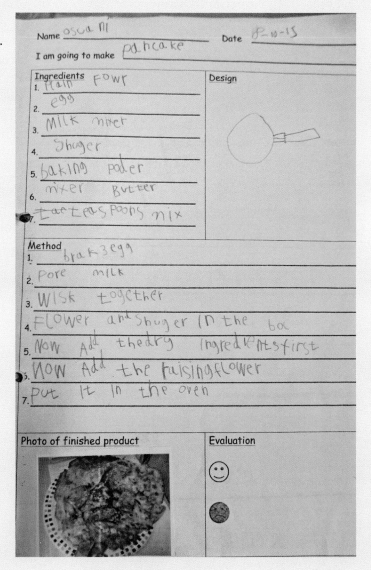

Diary extracts: examples of development and learning

WHAT TO LOOK OUT FOR

- Ground rules and expectations are established.
- The children are exploring the whole environment and using all the resources.
- The learning journeys show that the children are making progress in many areas.
- Teachers' files indicate good curriculum coverage.

Sand and cooking

In this diary section I am going to look at some events that happened in the sand and with the cooking units. One example has already been described in the September chapter. Efsun was pretending to cook in the sand and this led to real cooking indoors. This is a common pattern – much role play amongst young children is based around cooking and it is a logical, exciting and rewarding step to take this into real cooking in various forms.

There are so many examples of learning in these areas every day, the challenge is to just choose a few. As you read the book, you will see many more examples of learning in the sand area.

Lara noticed the Numicon in the sand and started stepping in each hole in turn. Rachel encouraged her to count with each step. Lara enjoyed the game and found all the pieces from one to seven. Lara was about to leave the area and Rachel reminded her to tidy up before she went. Lara hung the Numicon up in a random order and Rachel encouraged her to put them up in order from one to seven. Lara did this independently.

Sample learning journeys (see October chapter for explanation)

Identified Areas For Focus:

General/Parents:
'learn about giraffes'.

Curriculum:
* letter formation for g.
* time o'clock / half past.

PSCHE, RE
I imagine:- Literacy, D&T, art & design, music, PE
I understand:- Numeracy, science, history, geography, computing.
Consultation Meeting

Olivia and her friends were able to identify 3D shapes. ① introduced a game. Hide the shape in a box and describe it. ① encouraged to think about the number of sides. ① provide Olivia with shapes and encouraged her to look the sides.

Olivia watched a youtube clip on old and new aeroplanes. Olivia then drew a plane 'it's an old one because it has a propellor'. ① modelled the 'er' sound when she was writing what materials she needs. Olivia independently nailed pieces of wood together and cut pieces of wood to size to match her design. When finished Olivia wanted to write a story about her plane. ① encouraged her to think about the characters and setting. When writing the story ① reminded Olivia to say the sentence before she writes it. ① modelled letter formation for g. At circle time ① encouraged Olivia to read her story to the class and direct the actors.

Olivia drew a house and added it to a piece of paper. ① asked how we could connect all the buildings? 'a road.' Olivia helped to draw the road. Olivia experiment with moving the bee pot. ① modelled how to program the bee. Olivia was able to move the bee true movements at a time.

Outdoor Olivia helped to fit the piece to make 9 of a skeleton together. ① then provided her with labels with labels. ① supported Olivia reading words skull, spine, shoulder.

Olivia wanted to find frogs. 'where would they live.' 'in a pond?' ① suggested look carefully to see what lives. ② asks where she think they could see. 'look tadpoles'. Olivia seemed a little confused that tadpoles turn into frogs. ① encouraged read Olivia a non-fiction. ① then provided her with resources to help her sequence the life cycle of a frog. When she went back to the pond she said 'look froglets'.

Olivia brought a bear in from home. She spoke about ginger bread in front of the class. ① encouraged her to add him to the register. Olivia write his name using phonic knowledge. and then placed his name card on register board. 'I need to tick it so everyone knows he's here.'

Olivia asked ① to watch the monkey bars. She was able to move on 3 bars in one go. ① encouraged her to complete the whole course. 'look I did it. that was hard!'

Olivia took part in a maths activity on time. 'o'clock / half.' ① modelled where the longer would be. Olivia became feed with the numbers. ① than to do to just focus where the hand fold on the clock for o'clock and are positioned half past.

Olivia drew a giraffe and wanted to make it out of clay. ① encouraged her to look carefully at a giraffe in a book and include its features. ① modelled how to manipulate the clay using her fingers and tools. 'It's howel.' ① explained by adding a bit of water makes it easier to manipulate.

Olivia asked ① to make her teddy bears favourite food rice.' ① encouraged her to write the ingredients and method down. ① supported Olivia sounding out somewords. Needed ① reminding of the ai and er sound. Olivia then made the dish. she carefully cut the vegetables. ① modelled vocabulary that quartes. After it was cooked she shared it with her friends and teddy bear.

Identified Areas For Future Focus:

General/Parents:

Curriculum:
* Letter formation for g
* Applying diagraphs when writing
* Half past - time.

Year One Learning Journey For ..... Kai .... Autumn Term Date ...Oct.... Week ...3......

General/Parents:

✓ Develop interest in the police
Curriculum: mum: Learn to ride a bike at
the weekend.
Letter formation for a.

* Adding and Subtracting single
* digit numbers.

PSCHE, RE

I imagine:- Literacy, D&T, art & design, music, PE

I understand:- Numeracy, science, history, geography, computing.

Consultation Meeting

Kai decided to make a police gun. Drew design + made material list. ① Helped him to find the wood and showed him how to use a vice & drill (safely).

Kai wanted to have a turn with the bee bot ① explains that he would have to add a building to the map. I'm going to draw a Police Station. After finding. He drew a police Station. Station on to one on the internet. He stuck his the bee bot along the map and tried to move the road. ① modelled how to program the bee. He was able to program the bee to move at a time ① introduced it two steps at a time.

Kai wanted to make a police car. Made a map yesterday and decided to use the bee-bots ① talked about what a police car looked like & showed Kai a picture Kai made a covering for beebot with paper, for Kai put beebot car on his map and acted out the events of the journey. Used language like first, then and now to order the events. ① talked about what you do in a real emergency.

Kai was playing with a group of children throwing bean bags. ① suggested they throw the bean bags into hoops and add different points to each. Kai helped to set up the game hoop. He wrote a 4 on a white board bean. ① modelled the correct formation. After several attempts at throwing the bean bag into the hoop it landed in the four point hoop. He wrote over to the scoreboard and added his name. Score. He then got another four. ① encouraged counting on and then together ① modelled form four.

Kai wanted to write a story about a police man ① encouraged him to use his literacy book and make a mind map of the characters, setting and the shared what was going to happen. During the shared writing of the story ① encouraged Kai to use the song/letter cards to sound out words ① modelled letter formation for a. about writing on the lines. At one point ① pre-knew Kai how to not to know how to Sf ① a word and ask Kai how he could find out. 'I don't know'. ① introduced using a dictionary. 'can we act it out at story time?' ① encouraged him to make the characters costume. Q:What do police men wear? Kai found a book on the police. 'look I need a gun a hat, gloves, a jacket, hand cuffs. I've got some at home with a key' ① suggested they make what ①

Kai acted out his story at circle time ① encouraged him to think about how the Police would feel and behave in a haunted house with a Vampire.

'these nails are too long ① encouraged him to find shorter ones ① introduced the names of the tools and techniques hammer, drill, pilot hole. Kai used creative ideas to use paper + tape as part of decoration & design. He then made a belt + hand cuffs. He then evaluated his design by looking in the police book and realised he hadn't made gloves he independently went for material.

Kai then wrote what you should do in an emergency. He was able to sequence the events ① modelled how to sew fabric together and modelled how to b his measure how big his head is. 'I need a badge he drew the badge and attached it to his hat.' letter formation for g and encouraged Kai to write tricky words 'the and to.

Areas For Future Focus:

Science
experiments forces.

Literacy- Letterformation

music.

There is a copy of the cake making book in the sand area, along with a balance. The children regularly pretend to make the cakes, being precise in their method and balancing the scales exactly. They improvise for the ingredients, using conkers, shells, water and sand!

Sand is the perfect surface on which to practise number and letter formation. The fact that the marks can be smoothed away immediately is appealing to some children. The picture below shows Baran practising number writing (remember, no one has told him to do this – he has chosen to do it) and he welcomes the help from an adult. The improvement is clearly evident – no boring worksheets here!

The soft surface of the sand means that children are willing to challenge themselves physically without the fear of bumps and scrapes that might happen on the concrete. The roll bar is in the sand too (something that the children are familiar with from Reception), and is still popular.

The cooking units have been in use almost daily in Year One. The design sheet has been completed in each case prior to the food preparation and Efsun's example can be seen in the September chapter. A few examples of the tasty treats made recently are: cup cakes, slab cake, frozen strawberry creams, pizza, vegetable rice, fruit smoothie, gingerbread men, biscuits and apple crumble.

When Olivia was a focus child, she brought in her teddy from home and said his favourite food was vegetable rice. She wanted to make some for her bear. She completed the design sheet with ingredients and method, and then made the dish with her friends.

When pizzas were going to be made, the group had to decide which would be the most popular topping – a great opportunity to introduce a bar chart to show the choices and popularity of each. Once the pizza was made, another opportunity arose to revisit the language of 'half' and 'quarter' when cutting the pizza up.

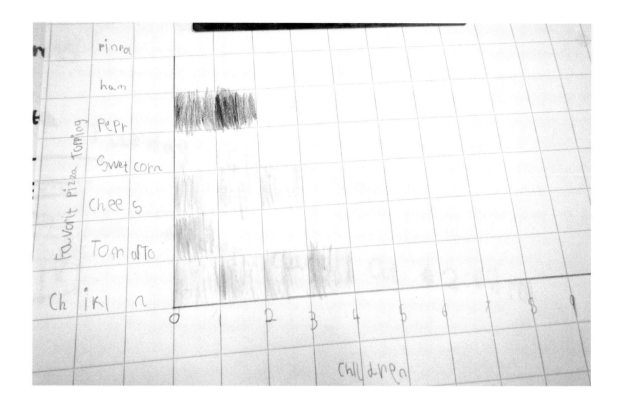

When Amira was looking at the globe and atlas, she started to look at the flags and also knew that some fruits come from far away. After a suggestion from Ruth, Amira wrote a list of fruits and where they came from. She talked about her mum making amazing things with fruit and went on to design a 'fruit person' on a design sheet. The next day she made her fruit person and the spare fruit was shared amongst the class.

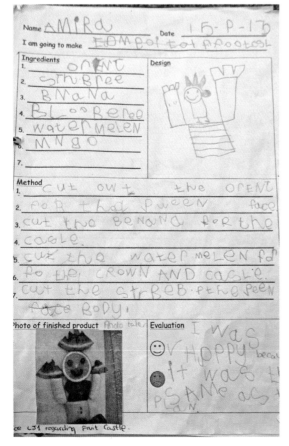

Learning journeys

For the second part of this diary section, I am going to look at sections of two learning journeys. In each case, although the child initiates the play, the adults are there to exploit the involvement and enthusiasm of the child to challenge and teach them in ways that are uniquely appropriate to that child at that time. This is what makes this way of working so successful – we are totally focused on the individual child in that moment, assessing exactly where they are at (academically and emotionally) so that the 'teaching' will be exactly appropriate and, therefore, in every case lead to progress.

The learning journey for Olivia (see page 46) shows the range and depth of her learning in all areas of the curriculum without any forward planning having been done. The environment in the school is superb and the adults are skilled at exploiting the teachable moments to maximise the learning potential in every situation. For example, after a video clip has been seen about aeroplanes, Olivia designs a plane to make. The video had shown an old plane and Olivia was able to apply this new knowledge when designing a plane to make. The adult is there to remind Olivia about the 'er' sound and some letter formation when she is writing on her design sheet. Olivia then makes the plane, measuring parts and considering shapes, using tools and evaluating the finished product. When Olivia writes a story about her plane, the adult takes the opportunity to introduce the terms 'character' and 'setting', etc. She also encourages Olivia to say each sentence before she writes it. When the story is acted out at the end of the day, Olivia is encouraged to read the story and direct the characters. This is just one entry on Olivia's learning journey and yet it covers aspects of literacy, design and technology, maths, history and computing. Olivia made progress in each of these areas of the curriculum – all triggered from one event.

The learning journey for Kai (see page 47) reflects his ongoing interest in police and fire fighters. In this instance he wanted to write a story about a policeman. Jacqui supported him with various secretarial aspects of the writing, as well as the compositional aspects. In order for the 'acting' to be realistic, Kai wanted a hat and was then introduced to sewing. He used reference books to help with the design and combined paper and fabric to finish the hat to his satisfaction. He went on to make a gun at the woodwork bench as well as handcuffs and a belt with other materials. Another part of the learning journey shows how Kai adapted the Bee-Bot to look like a police car and then used it on a map he had

made previously, programming the 'police car' to travel along the selected route to the police station that he had drawn. Kai had a wonderful week, totally absorbed in his learning, challenging himself to try new things, confident that the adults (and other children) would support him as necessary. Again he covered many different 'subjects' all through the vehicle of his interest in the police – literacy, design and technology, art and design, geography and computing.

The half term break is always welcome in schools – the first half term is often the hardest in the year. In Year One at Carterhatch, the staff have worked hard to ensure that each child feels valued and important. They believe that every child wants to learn and they understand that **learning can only happen if a child is not stressed or anxious**. Thus **well-being is always the priority**. Once these high levels of well-being have been established, then the learning happens. As explained previously, the environment, the timetable, the adults and the rules all have a part to play. The learning that has happened in this first half term shows that we have got most things in place to support high levels of well-being, involvement and therefore learning. The staff are all exhausted but also excited about the potential for the rest of the year.

3 November

November proved to be a very productive month in Year One at Carterhatch Infant School. The weather was wet, but mild, and the children carried on spending long periods outdoors. What was most noticeable for me was the independent learning that I saw. When visiting other schools, I am concerned about the level of 'control' that adults exert over the children. The children in these schools are missing out on the learning experiences that I witness every day at Carterhatch. Our children are creative, researching, exploring, taking risks, co-operating, making decisions, trying new things, experiencing defeat but carrying on, experiencing success and then finding new challenges. Possibly the most important benefit of this 'play-based', independent learning is the **emotional regulation and emotional resilience** that these children develop. When playing in a group away from an adult, planning, organising, negotiating, arguing and resolving disputes, the outcome is, in many ways, less important than the process. Through this play, the children are learning to regulate their own behaviour and emotions, and to get a conclusion that satisfies everyone and maintains their friendship group. **This life skill is proven to have life-long benefits**

and we must celebrate it again and again in order to not forget how valuable it is. The diary section will give just a hint as to the thousands of events that took place. With over 2,000 photos, the selection process was very difficult. In the first part of the chapter, I will describe the records that we keep for individual children and will also explain 'story scribing' and acting. In the environment section, I will look at woodwork outdoors. The diary section covers a range of entries: some new pets, some family/cultural/traditional events that led to activities in school, some mathematical learning that took place, some group events and also a couple of examples of story scribing. Each month I realise I could write a whole book for just that month!

TO DO LIST

- Re-establish expectations and ground rules after the half term break.
- Continue with the first cycle of focus children.
- Continue with the first cycle of parent meetings.
- Continue to monitor levels of involvement to assess the provision as a whole.
- Introduce one PE session per week per class.

Organisation

Individual folders

I have already stated this several times but it is easy to forget – **children in Year One want to learn**. However, they want to learn in their own unique way and through topics that interest them. If they write a letter, they do not want a sticker for their writing and they do not want their letter stuck in a literacy book. They want their letter delivered to the person it is addressed to and they want a reply! If they want to make a house for the fairy, they need to think about the shapes and sizes of the materials they are going to use.

Kiara is measuring this piece of wood because she needs a particular length for her model. This is not a maths exercise – this is maths for a purpose. The motivation (to create the model that she has designed) is far more powerful than any learning objective in a lesson about measuring.

Again, they do not want a sticker for their efforts and they do not want to write the measurements and shapes in a maths book. They want their house to look, and work, in the way they planned – so that the fairy will have a magical home. The levels of involvement are high – the children are all engaged in learning that is of interest to them and it is very practical and 'real'. Therefore, the children are happy; they are playing and through this they are learning.

However, as part of the senior leadership team, I am only too aware that we need to be accountable. We need to be able to show that we are meeting our statutory requirements in terms of curriculum coverage and we need to be able to 'prove' that each individual child is making progress. **We must meet the needs of the children AND the requirements of the curriculum and outside agencies.** However, we do not need to sacrifice one in order to satisfy the other – we can do both. We allow each child to pursue their own interests **and** we make sure that we track the curriculum coverage and progress of each child and the cohort.

We have given each child an A4 folder and everything to do with that child is in that folder (except highly confidential information). It therefore contains the following:

- a completed learning journey for each term (see October chapter for explanation);
- a parent sheet for each term (see October chapter);
- a 'special book' (see below);
- a curriculum book (see below);
- a 'writing' book (see opposite);
- any other items that the child or teacher wishes to include (art, photos of creations, etc.).

The **special book** is basically some A3 sheets of paper, stapled together and hole punched to go in each folder. The children can choose what to put in their special book: drawings, design sheets, photos, etc. If the book gets filled up, then we can simply add another one to the folder.

The **curriculum book** contains all the statements from the Year One National Curriculum. It is divided into subjects and the children or staff can add items to each section as evidence of coverage or attainment. The majority of the items added to this book are 'Wow!' observations from the staff. When they notice a child doing something independently for the first time, they will make a note of it, sometimes take a photo as well, and then add it to the corresponding section of the curriculum book. For example, Jemarly came up to Rachel and said 'Look ten and six is sixteen!'

Numicon is available in all areas of the environment. The children use it as a tool to support them in their pursuits. It is a resource to support learning. It is not kept in a cupboard and only used at specific times. It is always available and, therefore, when a child is ready to grasp a new concept, the resource is there to support them.

This was the first time that he had done this independently and was therefore noteworthy. Rachel took a photo, wrote a quick observation on a sticky label (this avoids having to re-write it later) and these were added to Jemarly's folder.

Once staff are confident that a child has attained a particular statement, they will make notes in the curriculum book (see photo on the right below). This is one of the jobs that the teachers can do in their PPA time. They are not having to do any forward planning (except for the phonic sessions) and, therefore, they can use PPA time to update individual folders. In order to keep this manageable, each teacher has a box file with a wallet for each child, into which they can drop photos and notes. This avoids hours of sorting through piles of photos – they are already sorted into each child's wallet.

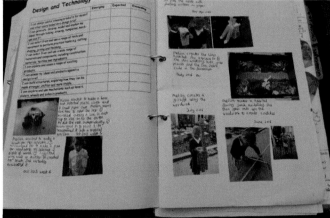

The **writing book** is an exercise book, hole punched so that it can be stored in the child's folder. In nursery and Reception, the children became used to 'writing' stories (to be acted out later – see the next section) on pieces of paper, so it is an easy adjustment for them to 'write' their stories in this book. However, all other writing is still done on paper (letters, shopping lists, etc.) or on design sheets. These (copies or originals) can be stuck into the writing book later or added at the back of the folder.

The folders are kept on low shelving in the classrooms so that the children can access them whenever they wish.
A copy of the curriculum booklet is available to download at www.creativecascade.co.uk.

The information in these folders is part of the evidence that teachers use when completing end of term assessments. However, the bulk of the evidence is in their heads. They know each child very well and can make assessments confidently and without the need to 'look up' evidence, since they can recall examples in every subject area. Staff who have switched to this more child-led way of working report that they have got to know the children in more depth and detail within one month, than they have done in a complete year previously. (See December chapter for more detail about assessments.) The most important feature of these folders is that each one is unique – no two folders are the same. Each child has experienced a year that is uniquely suited to them, their needs and their interests. However, each folder demonstrates both the outstanding progress that the children have made and that the whole curriculum has been covered. This is the proof that by playing, by following their interests, in an enabling environment, supported by skilful staff, children in Year One can make outstanding progress. **We can meet the needs of the children AND the requirements of the curriculum and outside agencies.**

Story scribing (and scribing in general)

Writing seems to be at the top of the list in most school development plans. If you have read my nursery and Reception books, you will know that our approach to all learning (including writing) is to keep it 'stress free'. We **never** force the children to write but we ensure that they understand the power and potential of writing. Thus **the adults *write for* the children** as often as possible. In this way, even if a child is not physically able to form letters, they can still see their thoughts and ideas transferred onto paper. This system continues in Year One where the developmental stages are even more varied. Staff continue to treat any writing as a shared venture with both the child and the adult contributing. This applies to their story writing as well. Whenever the staff feel it is appropriate, they will offer to scribe a story for a child. For example, when Rayan made this creation, Rachel approached him and said '**I wonder** what you have made!'. The use of the phrase 'I wonder . . .' is a great way to elicit a response from any child. It is a statement, rather than a question, and does not necessarily require a response. Therefore, it is not at all threatening and the child invariably responds.

In this example, Rachel then offered to scribe Rayan's story about events under the sea. When writing the story, it is important for the child to watch the adult write and for the adult to write exactly what the child says. In this way, even the youngest child learns that their spoken words can be transferred onto paper. They also see how writing is formed and what it looks like. The exact words that the child says are written down, even if grammatically incorrect. (See Appendix F for adult prompt sheet.)

As the year progresses and the children create more stories, then these transcripts become a record of the child's language and literacy development. For each child, the development will be unique, but with each story (or any piece of writing) that is scribed, the adult will be calling upon all their knowledge of the child and giving them opportunities to contribute to the process. This means that each child is challenged, but not overwhelmed by the task. In the atmosphere of trust that has been created, very few opt out – they all want to take the risk and attempt something new. For many children in Year One, the adults suggest that the children 'plan' their stories; deciding about setting, characters and events before they begin. To aid this process, we use a 'story mapping' sheet, as the example below shows. There is a blank mapping sheet in Appendix G.

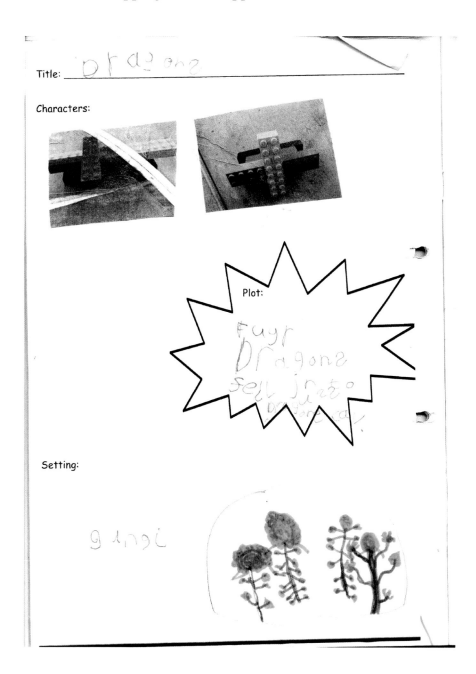

At the end of the session (morning or afternoon), the stories are shown to the group and an adult selects some children to act as the characters in the story. Then the story is read aloud and the children 'act' the story. When this activity is first introduced, and the children see a story being acted out, then many more of them will be keen to write a story the next day. As this is such a popular activity, some stories are acted out during the free-flow sessions and the stage is a great venue! Also, if a child can't find an adult to help with their scribing, they will often ask a friend to scribe for them.

The musical instruments are stored on a bookshelf next to the stage. With initial prompting from an adult, the children soon begin to add music to their story acting!

Setting up the environment

Woodwork area outdoors

Woodwork has the potential to promote learning in all areas and (as the picture opposite illustrates) delivers high levels of involvement. Although many practitioners (and parents) are worried about the risks, I would urge you to consider the **benefits** before dismissing this as a possibility in your setting. We have woodwork in our nursery and Reception classes as part of our continuous, outstanding provision. It is available all the time and (after the induction periods) it is not supervised by an adult (although the adults are continually scanning all areas of the provision). The same applies in Year One; the woodwork is always available, the children know how to use it safely and the benefits are huge.

'Risk assessments' by their nature, focus on the negative aspects of an activity. I always prefer to write a 'benefit/risk assessment'. In this way, we focus on why we are doing a particular activity before thinking about the possible risks and how to mitigate them. The benefit/risk assessment below demonstrates that the benefits of woodwork clearly outweigh the risks.

Benefit/risk assessment for woodwork

Benefits

Woodwork is the perfect activity in which children can demonstrate the characteristics of effective learning (these are taken from the Early Years Statutory Framework, but many schools are now using them to assess learning in all year groups):

- **playing and exploring** – children investigate and experience things, and 'have a go';
- **active learning** – children concentrate and keep on trying if they encounter difficulties, and enjoy achievements; and
- **creating and thinking critically** – children have and develop their own ideas, make links between ideas, and develop strategies for doing things.

In addition learning in all subjects is possible:

- *Physical development*: with the use of real tools and hard wood (rather than balsa wood), the muscles in the hands and arms become stronger and the children develop more control of these muscles. They learn to vary the amount of force used – with hammers and saws. They also develop hand-eye co-ordination in order to hit the nails. Fine motor control is developed as children hold the thin nails in place. Through experience they learn how to keep their fingers out of the way of the hammer. Co-ordination is developed as children learn to secure wood in a vice, hold a drill correctly, turning the handle and pressing down in order to drill a hole.
- *Personal, social and emotional development*: children demonstrate deep levels of involvement when undertaking a woodwork task. It is often noticeable that children who normally will not persevere at a task are prepared to try for far longer at woodwork – perhaps because they realise it is something truly challenging but also 'real'. Children will return to unfinished work the following day if necessary.

They learn to share and take turns, negotiating and discussing routines and rules. They learn how to keep themselves and others safe. They realise that a real hammer can do serious harm and they do treat the tools with respect. They learn to follow agreed rules. Children who find it difficult to conform are often so keen to participate, that they do manage to comply with requests and boundaries at the woodworkbench – just so that they get their turn. They take great pride in their achievements and therefore their self-esteem is boosted. For most children woodwork is a new activity and therefore they are taking a risk just by becoming involved – they take further risks using the equipment but learn to do this safely and independently and the results are greatly appreciated.

- *Speaking and listening*: there is always a lot of discussion at the workbench and therefore language is developed. Children have to follow instructions and will often be heard explaining the rules to other children. They encounter problems all the time and discuss solutions. They explain what they are doing and learn the vocabulary associated with the activity.
- *Creative development – including art and music*: with many activities for young children, the process is as important (if not more important) than the product. This is definitely the case when children are first starting at woodwork. They need to develop the techniques. Eventually, they will start to use their imagination, combined with their knowledge of the task, to plan what to make. With support, they will have learnt how it is possible to combine various materials and media and this will increase their options and possibilities. Many of the models become the starting point for a story which also supports creative development (as well as language and literacy skills). Musical instruments are also a popular creation and, by using real instruments, the internet and books for reference, the children in Year One can make accurate models and learn about music too.
- *Geography/science/design and technology*: clearly through working with wood, the children will learn about its properties and the properties of other materials that they combine with the wood. They will learn about how to use tools and how to combine different materials. With appropriate interactions, they could learn about the source of wood and various types of wood. They will be experiencing the process of 'design, make, review'.
- *Mathematical development*: this pervades every aspect of the task – from experiencing the weight and size of the wood to deciding how many wheels to add to a truck. Children will be thinking about size and shape, as well as number. Again, with appropriate interaction, their thoughts can be vocalised, refined and developed.
- *Literacy development*: children will often combine mark-making with woodwork – adding drawn features to their models. They also add their name to ensure their work is not lost. They will use books to refer to for ideas or information. Also, as mentioned above, many models will feature in stories and the literacy possibilities within this are infinite. In Year One, the design sheets (see Appendix H) mean that the children are writing titles, lists, instructions and reviews. For many children, this will be a shared writing process, but for all they will be learning about the features of these aspects of literacy.

This doll was made by Aleyna and is actually about 40cm tall. Once the doll was complete, Aleyna wrote a story with the doll as the main character. At the end of the day, when the story was read aloud, the doll took part in the acting.

- *History*: the techniques used at the workbenches have been the same for hundreds of years. Children begin to understand how objects are made and they try to replicate these processes. Many of the models produced are props to support stories or games. Reference books, or the iPad, are used and children then have access to images of objects from the past. This often leads to them making such objects and discussing the differences observed. (The use of the iPad for research introduces IT, as does the use of digital cameras to photograph the finished product to add to the design sheet.)

There are not many activities which appeal to so many children and have such broad and deep learning potential.

Woodwork – risks and actions

Hazard	Possible scale of injury	Precautions to put in place to reduce risk	Risk rating
General risk of injury through use and misuse of tools	Medium	Staff will ensure that children are closely supervised during the induction period until all children have been trained in the use of the tools and comply with the 'two children at each bench' rule. Staff will then remain vigilant in watching the woodwork area. Adults all aware of how to get first aid help if necessary.	Low

Hazard	Possible scale of injury	Precautions to put in place to reduce risk	Risk rating
Children with behavioural difficulties/ developmental delay might not adhere to the rules and might not use the tools safely	Medium	Staff will ensure close supervision of these children if they are near the woodwork area.	Low
Sawdust in eyes	Low	Children to wear goggles on windy days.	Low
Hit fingers with hammer	Low	Train children to tap lightly to fix nail in place and then move hand away when they hit harder.	Low
Children get hit by moving tools	Medium	Strict imposition of two children only limit at the bench. Staff will be scanning and monitoring the area at all times.	Low
Cut with saw	Low	Strict rule – 'wood in vice' to use saw.	Low
Splinters	Low	Wood will be checked. Children shown how to use sandpaper.	Low
Sharp nails cause injury	Low	Protruding nails will be hammered down. Children will not remove nails from work area.	Low

Clearly the benefits are great and the risks can be managed. (It should be noted that we have never had any serious accidents at the woodworkbenches and rarely have even minor incidents.)

Practicalities

- *Induction and access*: the bench is outdoors (the noise would be unbearable indoors) and in an area that can be seen at all times. Most of the children in Year One have attended our nursery and Reception and when they first started in the nursery, woodwork was available immediately with an adult beside the bench at all times during the induction period. In nursery and Reception, we encourage parents to help ensure that the children adhere to the very simple rules: two children at the bench, two hands on the saw. The induction period is much simpler in Year One, but the same process would be applied for new children joining the school. There is zero tolerance of any dangerous behaviour and the children quickly learn to behave appropriately if they want to be involved. The woodwork is part of our continuous, outstanding provision – it is always available and, therefore, does not cause a 'mad rush' to have a turn. Throughout the year, adults 'keep an eye' on the woodwork area, but an adult is not always 'stationed' there.

- *Equipment*: I would recommend small claw hammers, smooth fine nails (bought by the kilo from an ironmonger), adult-size hack-saws and hand-held drills. I have designed a workbench for schools and it is available from www.creative cascade.co.uk/products/wood-works/. It is sturdy and very reasonably priced. (See photo on page 60.) If the bench is not under a shelter, then cover it with a tarpaulin at night or in heavy rain.

- *Additional resources*: we add a variety of resources for children to fix to the wood such as milk bottle tops, elastic bands, fabric, corex, corks, string, etc. Paint, felt tip pens and pencils are available to decorate models as well. A good way to store these is in pots on an Ikea rail attached to the end of the workbench.
- *Wood*: wood is too expensive to buy. The best option is to find a local timber merchant who offers a 'cutting service' for customers. They are usually happy to keep off-cuts for use in school – we have taken a large bin to the timber yard which they fill up and we collect the wood every few weeks. The wood is stored on open shelving near the workbenches.
- *Design sheet*: as stated, we have a design sheet for use in Year One. Two examples can be seen overleaf.

Woodwork leads to deep learning and outstanding progress in all areas of development. Children are attracted to the challenges it brings and fascinated by the possibilities. Adults can be anxious about this activity but I would urge settings to have a go – the resulting engagement and learning will amaze and delight adults and children alike.

Name Klara Date 15.11.21	Name Hannah Date Sept 15
Design	**Design**

Materials and tools		**Materials and tools**	
1. Red ntil	4. Sar	1. wood	4. Sor
2. Wood	5. strin	2. scruis	5.
3. nails – hamma	6.	3. humer	6.

Photo of finished piece	**Evaluation**	**Photo of finished piece**	**Evaluation**
	☺ i lik t hami gn wood ☹		☺ ☹

Diary extracts: examples of development and learning

WHAT TO LOOK OUT FOR

- Children settle quickly after the half term break.
- Levels of involvement are high for nearly all children.
- Children display high levels of independence.
- Behaviour issues are minimal.
- Children work in groups – co-operating in their chosen learning.

Sample learning journeys (see October chapter for explanation)

Year One Learning Journey For ...Zipporah... Autumn Term Date 12.11.15. Week ....

Zipporah acted out her story in front of the class. ① encouraged her to behave like the characters when she spoke when she interacts.

PSCHE, RE

I imagine:- art & design, music, L

I understand:- Numeracy, science, history, geography, computing.

Consultation Meeting

Identified Areas For Focus:
General/Parents:

Curriculum:
* Story writing
* Number facts
* Computers - Program the beebot

Zipporah joined a group of chn making a zoo. She helped to place the animals in the different habitats. She was able to put the animals in their correct homes. ① Suggested She write the animals names to help the visit ors know which animals were in each area. She was ab Phonic knowledge

Zipporah wanted to make a clay Diya pot after learning about Diwali. ① showed how to model a clay ball and stressed being gentle once shaping. Zipporah made pot carefully and smoothed cracks to make a stable design. During making Zipporah and friends talked about their different religions. 'I'm a Christian.' ① reminded that the diya pots were for the festival of light. ① asked where you could get light from? Zipporah replied 'candles!' ① discussed less light in winter. Once modelled, the girls and Zipporah got tools to make patterns. Zipporah got upset as she didn't get the tool she wanted ① suggested swapping the tools after a couple of minutes, Zipporah showed took and got to by a range of mark m...

Zipporah was drawing a plan for a story she drew a magic door underneath characters. ① asked if that was going to be one of the characters in the story. explaining that the charact ers are who the story happen s to or who take part in the story. No that is where she puts all of her feet, Zipporah went on to draw her characters, her setting and plot. Zipporah began writing story. ① prompted to point by sound. Zipporah found a-o applied to two words.

Zipporah was able to write some high frequency words. ① asked Zipporah to use her phonic fingers to check go. 'Oh it's three digr Zipporah found er sound I. modelled capital I. ① with confidence

① encouraged her to discuss the book and talk about what she liked about the story

Zipporah read her reading boo h ① with

Zipporah wanted to make up a song with a dance routine. ② coaxed adult to write it for her. ① encouraged z to write it her self. ① called it 6 direction song asked to name her song when asked why she chose that name, she replied 'I like one direction that's why.' ① was able to think carefully with levels for her song. she coaxed for advice once Finished. she made up of dance routine with her peers ① modelled how to work out a simple routine using three movements. ② was looking forward to

Zipporah drew a picture of the guinea pigs. ① encouraged We'd look closely and add in details such whiskers. ① then suggested that Zipporah wrote down things she knew about the guinea pigs. She wrote what they eat what privilege. ① then encouraged how to use the pad to find out more facts (mummy) Zipporah used subtraction sums how to work backwards with adding (mummy) Zipporah used num ② how to subtract adding sums ② then ... how to ... How ... wild ① they guinea pigs live in ... (r) mild ① ... guinea pigs live ... where South

Zipporah took part in a PE lesson ① encouraged way move in different travel in different how ① modelled how to jump safely from the ③ name. Zipporah is very a-frame. Zipporah is very agile accessing PE

Identified Areas For Future Focus:
General/Parents:

Curriculum:
* Subtraction Sums
* Writing sentences and rereading work
* to check it makes sense

Performing to her peers at the end of the ...

Year One Learning Journey For ...Jemarly.......... Autumn Term   Date ..30.11.15. Week.........

Identified Areas For Focus:

General/Parents:

encourage positive relationships with other children - sharing, turn taking

Curriculum:

* develop reading - focus on pointing to words.

* number bonds to 10.

PSCHE, RE	
I imagine:- Literacy, D&T, art & design, music, PE	
I understand:- Numeracy, science, history, geography, computing.	
Consultation Meeting	

Identified Areas For Future Focus:

General/Parents:

See personal support plan.

Curriculum:

* finger spaces in writing

* reading - matching words to print pointing

Jemarly listened to T share the story 'Supertato.' T encouraged Jemarly to look at the cover of the book and think about the characters and setting. T supported J to identify the setting as the garden. J was very engaged in the story. He identified it had rhyming words but found it tricky to give an example of one. T modelled 'big' and 'strong.' Jemarly recognised the characters as looking like those in the Gruffalo.

Jemarly was hooping with his friends. T encouraged him to time how many seconds he could keep the hoop up. T modelled how to use a digital timer. J had a go - "3" he said. T modelled language "3 seconds." T encouraged J to make a scoreboard with his and his friends' names to record the number of seconds. J had a go hula hooping and timing his friends - T encouraged Jemarly to take turns and let his friends use the timer also. J kept saying "minutes" when reading the timer. T reminded him and modelled counting seconds on fingers.

Jemarly was interested in the book hunt after T shared it in reading. He wanted to retell the story. T encouraged him to plan and found it tricky identifying the initial sound of tricky words. T modelled tricky word "go." T encouraged J to find tricky word "we" from the card - he did. He could recite the words from the story himself. T encouraged him to find "ch" on the letter cards. Jemarly could write 'we' and 'go' from memory - next steps finger spaces.

They explained they have the same good ideas about what he could use. Jemarly gave a response to other children suggesting "no he wouldn't be a scaredy." J had lots to say. T encouraged him to listen to other children and wait his turn to speak.

Jemarly wanted to know how much money he had. He counted 2p and 1. T encouraged him to match his coins to numicon pieces. T modelled matching 2p. T encouraged J to count how much he had. "10p" he said.

J carried on playing with the numicon sandwiches. T encouraged him to make a number 7. "what is the matching number bond?" J matched number 3. "3!" T encouraged J to find different ways to make 10. T modelled writing there as number sentences. J then practised writing. T modelled formation of number 6.

Jemarly then played with the coins. He could identify a 5p number, which he did. He explored some other coins "5 + 2 = 10." T modelled putting 5. He counted on 2 more. J found this as a 5+5 number sentence. T encouraged him to check.

T encouraged him to add some. "Look in your head and count" this a little tricky. Later whilst exploring numicon J said to T "Look how 4 is smaller than 8." T encouraged J to count how T have lots of 8's. J encouraged "lots of 8, 8 × 8."

Jemarly brought a toy car from home. T encouraged him to make a road map that he had very been. He selected what he needed but it was very windy and the paper kept blowing a way. Independently he solved the problem by sticking it down on the table. T wondered whether his car was driving through town or countryside. "Countryside" Jemarly decided. T showed J an atlas with different landscapes and encouraged him to add details around his road. "Trees, I remember going there" he said. Jemarly added a forest of trees by drawing round his hand and some sheep which T modelled as he wasn't sure. T encouraged J to get a beebot - he needed some. Jemarly drive his car around the map using language like T modelled a 2 step instruction to turn and send the beebot to add a river into the river. T encouraged J to move it himself. He point the trees. "put the trees." T modelled putting the journey independently directing the beebot. T needed some support at first but completed half the journey the right way.

Jemarly was looking to change the date on the calendar. He knew it was soon. T encouraged him to tell me the month. "November." T explained it will be a new month tomorrow. J was unsure. T explained it will be December.

New pets

As stated, many of the children in Year One were in our nursery and they began to talk about the guinea pigs from nursery and how they would like to have some in Year One. Jacqui explained that pets cost a lot of money and that only the head teacher could authorise the expenditure. Several letters were then written and delivered to Adrienne and a reply was received the next day.

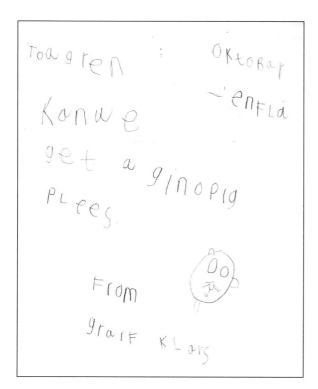

Dear Giraffe Class,

Thank you for your letter.

Please let me know how much guinea pigs cost and if he, she or they need anything else.

I will then look to see if we have enough money in school for you to buy some.

From

Adrienne

Adrienne

The children had no idea how much a guinea pig would cost and so they rang the pet shop and found out! They were shocked at the prices but, once they had the information, they wrote to Adrienne again.

Adrienne agreed to the purchase and therefore a large group of children went to the shop to select the guinea pigs and carry them (and all the accessories) back to school. The shopkeeper was very amused when the children offered to pay with their plastic money! Back at school, it was agreed that the guinea pigs would spend one week in each class and that the children in each class would clean out the cage before passing it to the next class.

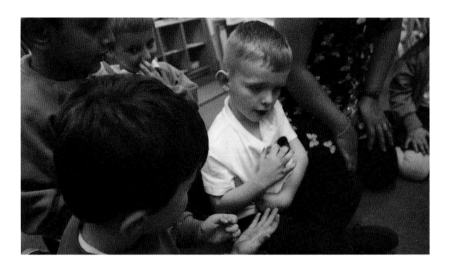

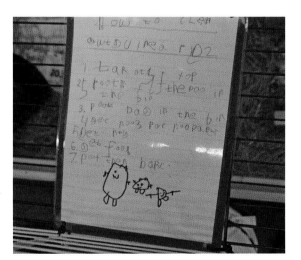

Malachai decided to write instructions to make sure that everyone did their job properly!

Diwali and bonfire night

This year Diwali fell in November, very close to bonfire night, with fireworks being used to mark both events. Several children were talking about these events and this led to discussions and art work.

The children in Year One come from a wide variety of cultural and religious backgrounds, with families celebrating numerous events. In many cases the children are simply aware that they wore special clothes, or that they had a special meal. What is important in any school is that all the children feel comfortable about sharing their experiences. Any setting develops its own 'culture' in this way because it is made up of many unique children, each with unique life experiences. One of the most important things we can do as practitioners is to develop within the group a culture of respect, acceptance, interest and enjoyment of the diversity. Beyond our statutory requirements, we do not become stressed and anxious trying to make sure that we mention and celebrate every cultural event during the year.

The details and facts about each child's culture are important to them – the atmosphere in which they are received in school is important to everyone.

Firework pictures were attempted by many children, trialling various techniques. 'Flicking' paint onto black paper was deemed the most successful by the group.

Diyas and rangoli patterns were also explored by the group.

Another event that occurred in November was Remembrance Sunday. A few members of staff and some children were wearing poppies. Zack was eager to explain how he had been at the church with his grandad. He drew a picture as he talked and Ruth scribed his words.

Mathematics everywhere

When children are given the freedom to learn in the way that suits them and via a topic that interests them, then everywhere I look I see maths happening. It is very difficult to avoid! To many, this is obvious, but unfortunately to many it is not at all obvious and needs to be explained. It is also easy to add items to the environment which will elicit further mathematical opportunities. We have seen how the children self-register by ticking their name on a list. With Numicon and a whiteboard pen placed close by, the children can record the total number of children in class.

In each class there is also a line of Velcro above '1st, 2nd, 3rd', etc. Each child has a 'mini-me' and they add their picture to the line in the order in which they arrive (thus covering ordinal numbers).

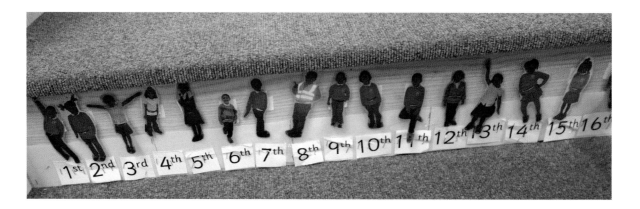

Whenever the children line up (to go for lunch, etc.), they are given a number card and then have to find the right position in the line – thus practising ordering numbers on a regular basis.

Money

You might have noticed from the photos that all the children have a 'money belt' around their waist. These bags contain money (plastic money!). In November, the amount is 10p each. The children might get ten 1p's or they might get a 10p piece and in this way the staff can differentiate the challenge. The children 'spend' the money during the day, putting their coins in the till and then taking whatever they have paid for. Most things in the creative areas are priced (indoors and outside) and the iPads are also available to rent!

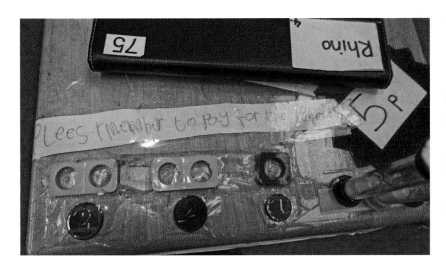

This sign says 'Plees rmember to pay for the iPad.' It costs 5p and the Numicon has been used to help the children work out how to create 5p using 2p and 1p coins. At this point in the year they have 10p for the day, so they have to be very keen to spend 5p on an iPad!

With the paper and collage materials priced at 1p or 2p per item, the stationery stock is lasting longer than ever previously known in Year One!

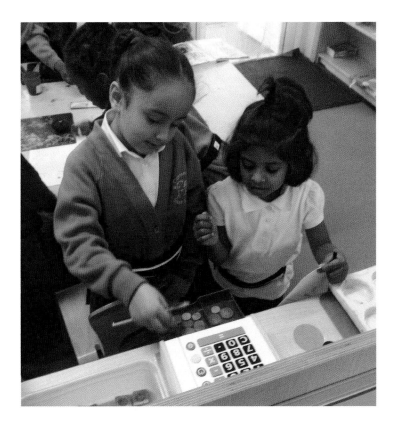

In every class, at any moment in the day, there are children discussing how much money they have, how much things cost, how much change they need, how to combine coins to make certain amounts, etc. In the outdoor area, the children are practising this new knowledge, playing with the giant coins and giant Numicon. (*Playing or learning? – both!*)

As mentioned earlier on, any child completing a piece of woodwork will have used mathematical skills throughout the process. Similarly, with cooking, which also happens on most days, the mathematical concepts pervade the activity. The adults often commentate as children play, in order to make the mathematical learning more explicit or to introduce vocabulary. When Jemarly was watching the children with hula hoops, he started counting to see how long they could keep the hoop going round. An adult suggested using a stopwatch, and then another child suggested recording the times on a board.

The children are still keen on playing the maths bingo on the iPads and are developing new strategies each day to work out the answers. Some children are using fingers, others Numicon, others number lines. Again the adults are around to commentate, make suggestions, offer resources and (when appropriate) challenges. Owen was finding the games very

easy and so the adult suggested that he try the next level (which involved multiplication). The concept was explained, using objects to group and count. Owen loved the challenge and persevered at the new level of the game for a long period.

Surfing

I'm not sure how surfing came into the minds of this group, but they were very serious in their endeavours to hold particular poses and to make sure they didn't fall in the sea. Eventually, however, they did fall and were eaten by sharks! An adult wondered if the boys knew where surfing took place in the world and the world map, along with an iPad, helped them discover the best surfing beaches in the world.

Go-karts have their tyres changed every two weeks and it costs about 50p per tyre to dispose of the old ones. So if you go to a go-kart track and ask for a few tyres you could end up with 500. A brilliant, free resource which can be used in numerous ways.

This world map is specifically designed for outdoors and, although quite expensive, it is sturdy and will not fade in the sun. It is permanently displayed outdoors and can, therefore, be referred to whenever an opportunity arises.

Building a zoo

Another group event that I saw this week was a zoo being built. When I wrote the nursery book, I included a group event when a house was built in the garden and this zoo reminded me of the atmosphere that occurred in the nursery two years' earlier. A large group working on one project, without any particular 'leader', without a written plan, with little (if any) adult input, leading to co-operation, new ideas, concepts developed and great fun had by all. As the game developed, the children decided to use various colours of k'nex to represent snow, water, sand, jungle, etc. Their discussions then revolved around where to place particular animals. They also decided to draw a 'map' as one of the group remembered being given a map when they visited a zoo. Extras, such as the toilets, 'ice cream shop' and 'hamburger bar' also became essential. Again, the idea of trying to distinguish between play and learning is ludicrous.

Story scribing (see page 58 for explanation)

There are stories being written in every class, every day. The starting point might be a game outside (police and 'baddies' for example), a model made at the woodwork bench, a drawing or just an idea. We have some beautiful 'small world' characters in the classes and these, too, are the inspiration for many wonderful 'traditional' tales. Adelle used the characters and combined them with some 'junk' modelling to create a story about a princess, a castle and a dragon. She took photos at each stage as she enacted the story and then used these to turn her story into a book. She insisted on making a tiny book for the princess too. As with every story, it was acted out to an audience – thus bringing the story to life.

Occasionally when I visit other schools, they report that the story scribing has not really 'taken off'. When I ask 'Are you doing the acting out?', they say 'Oh no not yet!'. The story writing will not be appealing unless the children know that their story will come alive through the acting. **Don't forget to act out the stories!**

Many of the boys, who enjoyed story scribing in nursery and Reception, are still keen to get involved with this activity. Their folders hold the evidence of their progress in writing. Several contain examples at the start of the year when an adult was scribing for them. Gradually the writing becomes a shared process and eventually the children write independently. Abdulkadir's folder is a good example of this progression and the two examples overleaf demonstrate the dramatic progress that is possible in the space of one month if the child is not stressed or 'forced' to write too much.

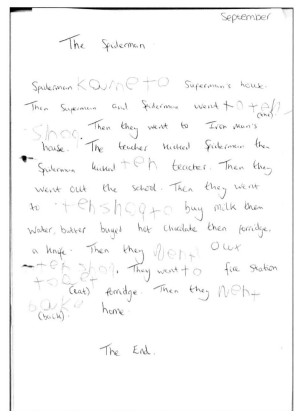

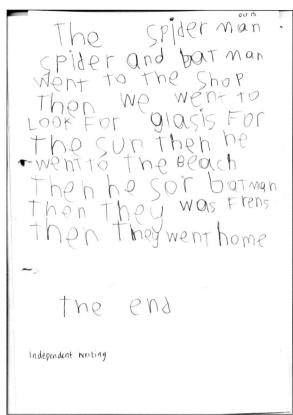

As November comes to an end, it is clear that the children continue to thrive within the structures, routines and expectations that we have established. As mentioned several times, our measure of success is the levels of involvement and whenever I walk through the Year One classrooms and outdoor area, I see high levels of involvement from almost every child. A closer examination reveals the vast array of activities that are taking place – football matches, cleaning out chickens, writing stories, designing models, building volcanoes, producing block graphs, baking cakes, singing and acting on stage, spending money to buy paper, researching 'Thunderbirds', reading a favourite story, having a snack, riding the bike, skipping, painting, transporting water through pipes, experimenting with salt on ice, etc. At any one time, there are 90 children engaged in their chosen activity – no one is bored, no one is stressed. As you can see, it is impossible to describe all these events in detail, but be assured that the examples shared in this book are not at all exceptional – they are the norm – just a taster of the wonderful learning that is happening every day. The individual folders, combined with the staff's knowledge of the children, show us that the children are making outstanding progress. This gives us the confidence to carry on with this child-led organisation of learning in Year One.

4 December

With daffodils appearing in December in 2015, it is interesting to teach children 'facts' about the seasons! As the Autumn Term ended, winter was not in evidence and Natasia's Autumn picture (above) seems to suit December. In this chapter, I will look at how Christmas found its way into Year One and will also look at the end of term assessments. In the environment section, I will look at how our provision supports physical development outdoors, as well as indoors, and the resourcing for art and design. The diary section will reflect these two areas of the environment, including a consideration of football and all the potential learning that can come from this interest.

TO DO LIST

- Complete first cycle of focus children.
- Complete first cycle of parent meetings.
- Discuss Christmas events and decide on end of term events.
- Join in with school end of term events as appropriate.
- Update individual folders.
- Complete end of term assessments (as required by the school).
- Review and evaluate the term – make changes for Spring Term if necessary.

Organisation

Christmas

As described in the November chapter, our main aims, with all cultural events, are to take the lead from the children and to ensure that there is a culture of tolerance and acceptance within school. Christmas is treated in the same way but almost every child in Year One was aware of the traditions, excited about presents, keen to get involved with decorations, eager to organise a party and happy to sing at the carol service. The team agreed that there would be resources and books available so that if children wanted to make cards or decorations, then they would be able to do so. A party was also organised, called an 'end of term' party, with food, dancing and games.

The resources in the creative areas were still priced and had to be 'bought'. Thus Melissa and Georgia calculated carefully how many pieces of paper to buy in order to make their paper chains.

Rayhan found a felt pin cushion appealing in the craft book and persevered to complete the design sheet and then master new skills – drawing templates, sewing, combining materials – to complete the task.

Sumaia was equally determined to complete her model

The quality of the stitching around the edge of this pin cushion is superb. Sewing is another activity that is continuously available. Because of this, there is no 'mad rush' to have a turn. The children know that the equipment will be there whenever they want to sew something.

of Father Christmas. She completed her design sheet, bought the resources that she needed and then worked with perseverance to finish the product independently.

The children in Year One joined the children in Year Two to sing some carols to parents. They learnt the songs over a period of a couple of weeks during group sessions at the end of the day and then had a few rehearsals in the hall with Year Two. The atmosphere was relaxed and nearly all the children were confident to join in. This was one event that was not child-initiated and one other surprise event took place as well. Rather than pay for an expensive, professional show, I persuaded the Year One staff that we should perform a pantomime of 'Snow White'. The two head teachers, office staff and various others all joined in and (without any rehearsals) put on a fabulous show. Once the rumour went round school, every class wanted to watch and so the audience was far bigger than expected. A great way to end the term!

I bet at least one reader is panicking because this model looks like it might have been made with a toilet roll. Well it has! And anyone worrying about this needs to look at the Health and Safety Executive website and, in particular, their 'myth-busting' page which states that it is fine to use toilet rolls as long as they don't look contaminated!

Assessments

As explained in the November chapter, each child has an individual folder and staff use these, combined with their vast knowledge of each child, to complete any assessments. At the time of writing this book, we are in a time being referred to as 'life without levels' in which schools are developing their own ways of tracking progress between statutory assessments. We are required to state whether children are below, at, or above 'expected' levels – except no one is really clear about what that 'expected' level is. All very confusing. Schools are buying various tracking programmes and assessing children against hundreds of statements. In 2015, we decided to track all key indicators in literacy and maths. This data was entered into a computer tracking system in order to be able to 'pull out' information about 'groups' (summer born boys, for example). This does not support individual children – it is to provide evidence in order to be accountable. Staff were also aware of general progress in other areas of learning, based on their knowledge of the children. Also, 20 per cent of the year group were assessed in maths, using a commercial test. They were tested at the end of Reception and then twice more during Year One. We also had numerical data about phonics and reading levels. With any tracking system, the information provided tells us very little about any individual child but does give an indication of broad progress for individuals and for the cohort. This is another task that we do to meet the requirements of outside agencies but which does not benefit the children. It is ludicrous that we are told over and over that each child is unique but then we can group them according to gender, ethnicity and numerous other categories. The unique child suddenly disappears!

The data produced at the end of the Autumn Term showed that almost every child had made good, or better, progress (assessed against the key indicators). The maths assessment (of 20 per cent of the cohort) showed that all, except one child, had made expected, or better, progress. One third of those assessed had made over 17 months' progress in the first term in Year One! Each teacher met with the head teachers for a progress review. In the few cases where the children had not made expected progress, the teachers knew the reasons and could explain these with confidence. However, I do not need numerical data to tell me that what is happening in Year One is beneficial for the children. I see it every time I go into the classes and the garden. The children **love** being at school, they display deep levels of involvement, they are laughing and talking, they are co-operating, persevering, taking risks and learning at every moment. Only a fraction of this can be measured numerically and we must resist the temptation to focus on the tiny parts of the curriculum that can be measured in this way. Of course, literacy and numeracy are important, but it is their application that will inspire children to love learning.

Setting up the environment

Physical development

Children are developing their physical ability from the moment they get out of bed – getting dressed, walking, cycling, skipping, running or hopping to school, moving around the building, etc. However, in this section, I am going to describe how we have set up the environment to support the physical development of the children.

The photo opposite gives a good view of the run of monkey bars that we have installed in the Year One area. Monkey bars, rope swings and trapeze bars are the only fixed climbing equipment that I would advocate. It is very difficult to develop upper body strength without this sort of equipment and if it is not available in an outdoor

area, then this is when the use of the hall for PE might become necessary. In the October chapter, there is a wonderful photo of the roll bar, which also helps develop the gross motor skills of the children. A-frames with a single pole work equally well (see suppliers list in Appendix I). I once taught a girl who was paralysed down one side of her body. The exercises given to her by the occupational therapist did not appeal and she refused to do them. However, she wanted to master the monkey bars and spent up to two hours every day pushing her weak arm up and then swinging from the bar. By the time the therapist returned three months' later, this girl was able to travel across five bars! That is the power of child-initiated learning – if it is something that they have chosen to do, then they will persevere and challenge themselves to do things far beyond what we can imagine.

We have two-wheeler bikes, confined to a small L-shaped area. As with all activities, we assess its value by monitoring the levels of involvement. I do worry when I see trikes in Reception as the children do not have to concentrate at all in order to ride them. This is definitely the case in Year One – trikes would not be appropriate. The two-wheeler bikes offer challenge to the children and the shape and size of the space brings further challenge – turning around in a narrow space without putting your feet on the ground is very difficult, even for the most experienced rider.

The plan of the outdoor area on page 14 shows that there are two large open areas – one is used primarily for football (discussed in more detail in the next diary section) – but it is also used for basketball, hockey or netball as we have attached a ring to the wall to 'shoot' at. The other area is used for various activities using the PE equipment stored on this trolley. There is also a large whiteboard nearby as well as clipboards and pens so that individual names, times, scores, distances, etc. can be recorded.

These girls have collected some crates from the large construction area having experimented and found that the extra height helped them turn the rope more successfully.

In the November chapter, I described the **woodwork** that is on offer and this, of course, develops the physical abilities and co-ordination of the children. The large growing area also requires physical skill from the children – digging the area, pulling up weeds, etc. and this area is described in more detail in the February and May chapters.

As mentioned, the classes each have one PE session in the hall each week. This term the sessions are being used for gymnastics and the children are able to apply all the skills that they have developed in their outstanding early years. They are confident and keen, willing to take risks and try new things, but also able to assess risk and behave sensibly on the equipment. We use a system whereby half the class are in the hall and the other half go to the library, and then they swap. This means that the staff (the teacher and a specialist learning support assistant) can concentrate on just 15 children in the hall at any one time.

Creative and physical development

Outdoors and indoors there is creative equipment available (at a price!) and it is through creative endeavours that much fine motor physical development takes place. The diyas described in the November chapter are a good example. Clay is always available and finger strength, dexterity and control are developed as the children struggle to complete their models. There is no need for 'fancy pants' programmes, such as 'dough disco' to inspire children. They have wonderful imaginations, they want to get involved and they will develop these skills if the opportunities are given to them.

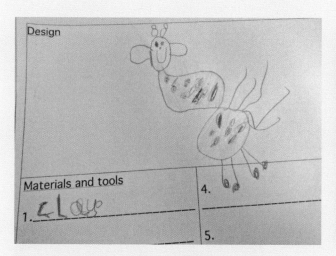

Drawings, such as this, are a good indication of the physical development of a child. If a child is struggling to make firm marks on paper, then they should not be pushed to do this if they don't want to. However, working with clay will develop the hand muscles and lead to improved pencil control. It is this sort of information that needs to get through to literacy co-ordinators and head teachers.

In addition, there are all the usual things available in the creative areas – coloured paper and card, collage pieces, various mark-making implements – pencils, pens, crayons, paint, chalk, various types of glue, junk modelling, etc. Everything is available for the children to self-select – the tables are empty at the start of the day and there are no pre-defined learning objectives. The children decide what to make and how to make it; they complete a design sheet and then select (and pay for) the items that they need. There are craft books in each class and these are used for reference and information about specific techniques or as a stimulus for ideas of things to make.

In addition we have a sewing 'trolley' which can be wheeled into any room where it is needed and this is what Rayhan used when making his pin cushion (see page 83).

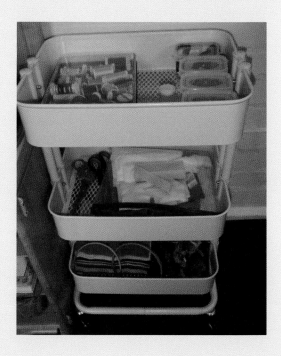

Diary extracts: examples of development and learning

WHAT TO LOOK OUT FOR

- Children working in groups – independently from adults.
- Children becoming fascinated about the 'logic' of numbers.
- Parents pleased with first term in Year One.
- Data shows outstanding progress is being made by most children.

Family items

Elvire brought in a photo showing some family members in traditional Congolese dress and she wanted to make a similar item. This was the motivation which led to physical development for several children as they worked together, cutting paper, sewing fabric, applying glue accurately, etc. Elvire was delighted with the result.

Sample learning journeys (see October chapter for explanation)

Year One Learning Journey For ...Cinar...... Autumn Term Date ...02/12/15. Week ....1...

Identified Areas For Focus:
General/Parents:

Curriculum:
★ Become more interested in drawing
   - recently → encourage use of different techniques & media
★ Encourage capital letters / full stops
   in writing & independence.
★ Use counting (on) method in sums.

Cinar exploring with 3D shapes. ⓣEncourage Cinar to count the corners. ⓣAsk Cinar to name the different shape. Cinar recognised cylinder, cube and cuboid. ⓣhelped Cinar to recognise cone and prism. ⓣTalked about halves and quarters. Cinar drew different shape and cut them in halfs and quarters. Cinar find out that some shape cannot be cut in quarters. ⓣ explained about symmetry. Cinar also counted the line of symmetry. ⓣAsk Cinar for remembering his shape.

Cinar was playing maths Bingo addition. Cinar kept getting stuck because he was rushing with the counters. ⓣencouraged Cinar to use two fingers to do simple sum like 5+3=8 7+2=9 etc Cinar was more confident using his fingers. ⓣben encouraged Cinar to put a big number in his head and count the other number on his finger ie 9+4=13. Cinar became more confident and started to play independently even with harder sums. ⓣPraise Cinar.

Cinar looked through the cook book. Cinar wanted to make ginger bread house. ⓣEncourage Cinar to write a plan. Cinar wrote the ingredients and the method. ⓣReminded him about capital letters/full stops, ⓣPraise Cinar for trying so hard. ⓣexplains the shape be nose is going to be. So ⓣ modells the nose out of paper. Cinar makes a template for his house. After making the dough, Cinar uses his templates to cut out his six squares. After cooking Cinar and ⓣtried to put it together but it kept falling apart. Cinar "we needed to make it more thick" ⓣ"yes the icing" Cinar still enjoyed his biscuit.

Cinar and friend looks through the science book and wants to make a paper plane. ⓣhelps them select a good material for the plane. ⓣexplains the different plans of making aeroplane. Cinar tested out the paper & error... aeroplane outside. ⓣ talked about the direction of the wind and gravity. ⓣalso advised how if he threw the aeroplane up right it goes further. ⓣ encourage Cinar to measure how far the plane went. Cinar used tape measure ⓣencourage Cinar to record his findings. ⓣhelps him read it and helps him to write 3 digit number. Cinar "I won." ⓣ"yes, because you threw it up right ⓣ

Cinar wanted to write a story on a dragon. ⓣ encouraged Cinar to write a plan. Cinar told me the names of characters & took picture of the lego characters. ⓣhelped Cinar to write a plot and the setting of the story. Cinar then wrote the story by himself. ⓣreminds Cinar of full stops and writing on the line. ⓣreminded Cinar of "ai" and "sh" diagraphs. ⓣreally emphasised the sound...

In library with ⓣ reading a story in character." ⓣasks q's about characters & setting. ⓣable to answer some q's ⓣprompts him to explain more using story to help him e.g. "Why did they all done?, etc ⓣ modelled drawing on the story & using pics to help him find answers & understand stay more ⓣ was able to comment on what he liked & why.

PSCHE, RE
I imagine:- Literacy, D&T, art & design, music, RE
I understand:- Numeracy, science, history, geography, computing.
Consultation Meeting

Cinar in P.E. in hall exploring different equipment. ⓣmodelled & encouraged ⓒ to see think of different ways to travel along or over the equipment. ⓒexplored different climbing techniques & jumps e.g. bunny hops along bench, pencil jump off of table bench. ⓣ supported by encouraging feet together when jumping, bending knees. ⓒvery confident & capable moving on equipment.

Identified Areas For Future Focus:
General/Parents:

Curriculum:
★ Has become more interested in writing, encourage spelling & simple punctuation
★ Draw on own history & compare, ⓣ told & plan items e.g. toys

Year One Learning Journey For ...Nadir...

Identified Areas For Focus:
General/Parents:

Curriculum:
- applying phonic sounds he knows in sanding out to read
- Segmenting to spell.
- ✓ Concentration in group time

Nadir
"I want an ipad" (T)Explains Pay 5p. (N)Says I don't have a 5p. (T)wonders how he can make 5p using other coins. (N)looks @ coins (N) said value of coins. 2 + 2 makes 4 (T) wonders what he needs to make 5? He says "2 + 2 + 1" and he finds using money.

Nadir was @ phonics area, games looking @ word making board. (T)explained how to look @ p.c. say what it is & sound out to put sounds in order to make. (N) Saw snork & sounded out correctly but put 'ch' instead of 'sk'. (T)emphasised 'sk' sand & did action. (N) looked again & changed to 'sk'. (N) made other words (T)had to emphasise & support with some of the digraphs.

Nadir filled tub with small lego pieces and held microscope on top of them. Nadir says "Look at my find a scope"

(T) models sentence "look at my microscope" Nadir repeats sentence and correct word when (T)modelled. (N) began talking to his peers. YH.

Nadir wants to make ginger bread house with friends. (T)encourage Nadir to write a plan. Nadir writes the ingredients. (T) really emphasise Sounds for Nadir. He writes ingredients and gets tired and doesn't want to write method. (T)models a house out of card. Nadir watches and makes a template for his ginger house. After cooking the biscuits Nadir and (T) put it together. Nadir "It is not sticking." (T) "yes, maybe we needed to eveluate plan. Nadir to evaluate plan. Nadir really enjoyed the ginger bread house. (TB)

Nadir Exploring with 3D Shape. (T)encouraged Nadir to name them. Nadir knew a cube and sphere. (T)encouraged Nadir to count the sides and edges. (T)explained the rest of the 3D shape

Nadir listened and then was saying it when he was making a tower. Nadir then was drawing shapes with a friend Nadir "you can cut this in half (T)can you cut it one more time. Nadir "yes" (T)yeah then it will be a quarter. Nadir then drew other shapes and was trying to cut them in halfs and quarters. (T)explains you cannot cut all the shapes. (T)talks about shapes that are same but diff. Nadir shows a square "this is similar & praise (TB)

(N) brought in his octonauts toy to show class. He then said he wanted to write a story using them. (T)introduced planning form etc and encouraged (N) to write ideas for characters/setting & simple plot ideas. (N) needed support to not run the words he was writing and to take time in segmenting to hear sounds.

(N) was looking @ a non-fiction book on mountains. (T)explained how has real info in. (N) found a page where showed has (T) read instructions to plan & find resources. (T) introduced paper mache technique (N) made mountain how to do. (N) made maintain & painted. He said I want to leave at school so feet together & head everyone can use it. Knees. (N) got v exc & enjoyed exploring the different apparat

PSCHE, RE

I imagine: Literacy, D&T, art & design, music, PE

I understand: - Numeracy, science, history, geography, computing.

Consultation Meeting

(N) was looking @ my microscope Beebot (T)explained what it does & (N) got very excited. (T)modelled how to use YH.

(N) to input own instructions for the Beebot to follow read our map. (N) needed reminding not to do too many instruction at once & to clear (instruct wise it will keep doing Same thing. (N) understood the Smart programming.

(N) was in P.E. explaining to travel around safely & (T)explained how modelled different technique to move along, our low equipment eg. bunny hops, pencil jumps etc. (N)tried to bunny hop along the bench with (T) reminding to keep

Identified Areas For Future Focus:
General/Parents:

Curriculum:
- To look at simple science experiments where he tests out ideas.
- To discuss own history/events from past using own old photos/toys etc

There are examples of art and design throughout this book – it is one of the best vehicles for learning in all subjects. As Elvire completed this project, she had covered art, design and technology, physical development, history and geography (discussing Congolese traditions), language and literacy (discussing and completing the design sheet), maths (aspects of shape, space and measure), as well as numbers and money when buying the resources that she needed.

As mentioned, in the Autumn Term we asked the focus children to bring in some items from home. Many of them brought in photos taken at various points in their life. Rachel wondered if Sasha could place the photos in chronological order. Sasha did this and then put her baby shoes next to the photo that was taken at the time that the baby shoes would have been worn.

Creative projects

It would be easy to fill a book with the art and design work that is happening each week in Year One. Rather than describe the events in detail, I am including some photos that were taken within just two days in school. I could have included many more but just want to illustrate that the examples in the book are in no way exceptional; they are the norm. As you look at each one, keep in mind that no one told the children to make these things. They chose to make them (for various reasons) and did so with minimal instruction or support. They each asked for help if they needed it, many of them working with friends and getting their help before asking an adult. Consider, also, the learning that occurred during the process or during discussions.

Melissa's worm house

Alara's symmetrical printing

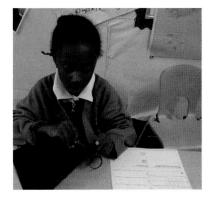

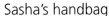

Sasha's handbag

Austin's bike

Alfie's rocket   Ronaz's doll   Cinar and Wiktor in their glasses

As mentioned, many children are working in groups and one example of this was **a gingerbread story**. Some children were talking about how they always have gingerbread biscuits at this time of year. Others started chanting 'You can't catch me, I'm the gingerbread man!' Skylar decided to design and make a gingerbread man but when she looked in the cookery book, she found images of a gingerbread house and this was even more appealing. With ideas from the book and some suggestions from Rachel, the children designed the house, cut templates out of paper for the various sections of the house, made the biscuit dough, cut and cooked the shapes and stuck it all together with icing when it was finished. They then had great fun decorating it (having written a shopping list and bought the essential sweets!).

Skylar also wrote a story involving a gingerbread house and this was acted out with a few children forming the 'house' during the acting of the story (see November for story scribing). Later the group enjoyed smashing the house into pieces (as described in the story) and then eating it!

Football

Some visitors this month saw some boys playing football and expressed a concern that some boys would not do anything else if they are given the freedom to choose what to do. I returned to the outdoor area after these visitors had left and the same group of boys had obviously become exhausted after their game and they were all indoors writing a report of the match. Once I started to think about this ongoing passion for football, I realised that we are gaining a great deal of learning from this initial stimulus.

Nearly every day a group of children rushes outside to play their daily match. The first task, if there are a lot of children wanting to play, is to sort out who is going to play.

The staff have provided a limited number of jackets (thus limiting the numbers that can play) to be used on such occasions. This involves negotiation and discussion but the group will do this without calling on an adult. If only a few children want to play, then the jackets are not needed. The children have devised a system whereby anyone without a jacket can sit with the timer and will get a turn when the timer is finished. Often, one child will collect a clipboard to keep notes and scores as the game is played. The next task is to mark out the pitch using large blocks of chalk. Therefore, before the game even starts the children have been speaking and listening, using a timer, writing on a clipboard, drawing the lines for the pitch (this, again, involving discussions and concepts of size and shape).

When playing the game, they demonstrate high levels of involvement, develop their physical skills and co-ordination, continue to communicate and co-operate. They rarely call on an adult – it wastes too much time – they have learnt to negotiate without anyone becoming upset. Adults do get involved for other reasons and this is where the potential of the game can be expanded. For example, the group were discussing various teams and then looked at an atlas to see where these teams came from in the world.

Kevin also used the iPad to look up information about some teams and then came across photos of teams from a 'long time ago'. He was fascinated by these and asked for some of them to be printed so that he could stick them in his folder. He then went on to draw some football players and was reminded by an adult that the players all have numbers on their shirts. He was keen to add this detail to his picture.

When looking at his drawing, Kevin noticed that the hands looked like '+' symbols and wondered what all the numbers would add up to. Thus the Numicon was introduced to do this calculation.

On this same day, Demar, and a group of friends, made a football cake, designing it carefully and using icing to mark the lines – repeating the line marking from the playground but on a much smaller scale.

The writing about the match was written in a commentary style, and although Osuani was the instigator of this, the whole group were keen to have this writing in their folders. They helped each other, applied their phonic knowledge and persevered for over half an hour to complete their task, with a detailed drawing added as well.

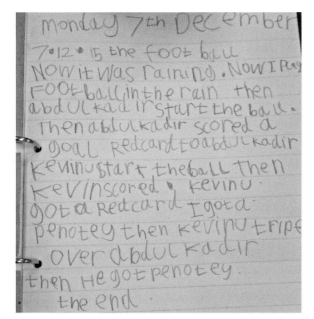

Another group attempted to make a 'table football' game that they had seen when on holiday. Again the iPads were used for reference, a design sheet completed and then the model was made by a group of football enthusiasts.

What is very interesting is that the boys who are skilled at football are also skilled at other things too. Also they do not play football all day – they would get too exhausted. However, when they leave the match, they find something else to do that is equally engaging and this often has a football theme. But the learning continues and the few examples seen here are evidence of this.

At the end of the Autumn Term, the children and the staff are exhausted but they are happy. They have had a wonderful first term, with everyone working so hard to make this year a success. The adults have created a physical environment that is able to cope with having 90 children free-flowing and engaged. They have also created an emotional environment in which the children feel empowered to take their learning in any direction and to any level. The children know that the adults will support them, without taking over, and thus they seek help as they need it. The data shows that the children have all made good or accelerated progress, the levels of involvement remain consistently high and therefore the team do not see any need to alter the structure or routines of the day in the Spring Term. Exciting times ahead!

5 January

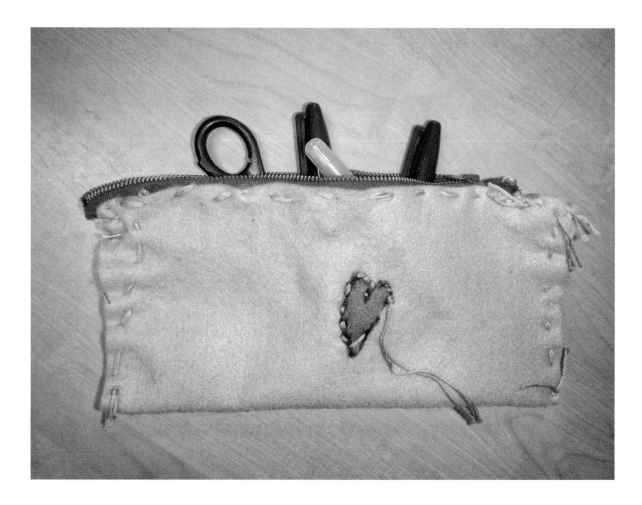

As 2016 begins, the children return to Year One at Carterhatch as eager as ever to learn. The staff team have been reflecting on the organisation of the year group and have decided to make a few minor changes to the environment and these are described on the following pages. In addition, with the new term the team have devised a new 'focus child' sheet to go home to the parents and this is also explained in this chapter. In the environment section I will describe the changes that have taken place in Giraffe class as a result of the new organisation indoors and will look at the stage and music area outdoors. The diary section will give some examples of the learning from Giraffe class as well as a snapshot of the continuing exciting learning outdoors.

TO DO LIST

- Start second cycle of focus children.
- Start second cycle of parent meetings.
- Implement changes as identified from the review of the Autumn Term.
- Support some of the children to make self-assessments.

Organisation

A4 learning journey sheets

At the team meetings, the staff decided to reduce the size of the learning journey sheets for the focus children (see October chapter for explanation of these). In the Autumn Term, these were A3 sheets, but staff are finding that the children are now pursuing one activity for such a long period that it would be better to have smaller sheets with fewer entries. They recognise that it is the 'teaching' that is important, rather than the record on paper. They are also skilled at picking out the critical **teaching** step in the long process that is needed on the learning journey. Thus the examples in this and the next few chapters are A4 size and the time and complexity of the activities is evident.

Specialist areas

The staff have seen how confident and independent the children are and so have decided to allow them to free-flow into all the classrooms. Until now, they have been mixing out-doors, but mainly staying in their own base indoors. With this change it means that they no longer need to have all resources available in all classrooms. Each class has therefore been given a 'specialism' to have in their room, along with the basic provision which will remain in each room. The three specialisms are: art and design (see the environment section in this chapter for details), science (see February chapter) and cooking (see March chapter).

Telling the time

Another change is the focus child sheet that goes home to parents. We have set up an email address specifically for the families in Year One. The new sheet that the children take home explains that during their focus week in the Spring Term, the parents can email in some photographs from home. The sheet has also been amended (see Appendix J) to include an introduction to clocks and time. A completed parent sheet is shown below.

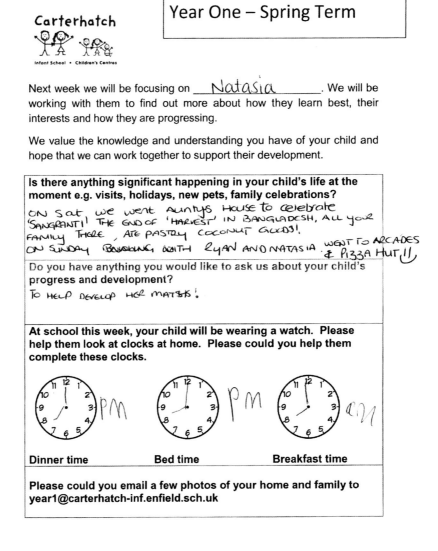

In addition, we have purchased watches and the focus children will wear a watch for their focus week at school. We have also bought a stock of watches for parents to purchase for their child if they wish. Telling the time is one of the things in the Year One curriculum that we feel is inappropriate but which we accept that we have to cover. Having taught in Key Stage Two, and from my experiences as a parent and foster carer, I know that it is easy to teach a child to tell the time in Years Three or Four. However, we are going to do our best to teach this in Year One in a practical and meaningful way. Therefore, the focus children will be responsible for the time-keeping of the class during their focus week. Adults will support them to tell the time and to relate this to events throughout the day. The watches that we have purchased include indications of half and quarter, to support this learning. We have also placed two giant outdoor clocks in the outdoor area and the clocks indoors are at the children's eye level to encourage their use.

It is important that adults understand that learning happens everywhere, all the time. The children who opt to be outside do not miss out on any curriculum coverage as the staff have ensured all subjects are resourced, both indoors and outside.

Self-assessments

One other change that has been introduced is to encourage more children to make self-assessments against the statements in their folders. Jacqui, with help from the children, has organised this area so that the children can take photos and write short observations of their own work.

Thus Giovana recorded her efforts with skipping and counting backwards and then added the photo and observation to the maths section of her profile document.

Class monitors

In an effort to further increase the independence of the children, the staff are allocating 'monitors' for each class – ensuring that every child has a turn in this role. These children wear a 'hi-viz' jacket for the day and are responsible for ensuring that the children remember the class rules. Thus they can be heard reminding children calmly and consistently that they need to walk indoors and tidy up areas when they have finished. They are also supervising their peers as they walk around the school. Fines are being introduced for anyone who runs or shouts in the corridors – 1p seems to be the agreed amount!

Setting up the environment

Specialist creative area

We have three classrooms in Year One and with the re-organisation the children are now able to go into all the rooms. Giraffe class has been designated as the 'creative/art and design' room, although each room still retains the basic mark-making equipment. Giraffe class now has all the sewing equipment permanently available, along with clay, collage and all the items as described in the December chapter. The work being produced is of a very high standard, a sample of which is described in the following diary section. The design sheets are also in this area, and an example of a completed sheet is shown below. A blank design sheet is shown in Appendix M.

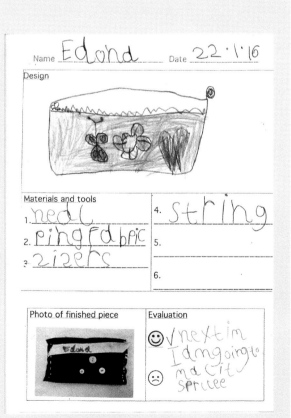

Music and stage area

This stage has been built from the discarded lids from some small sandpits. If you have such sandpits, this is a very good use for the lids and the sandpits can be covered with tarpaulins if necessary. Another simple and cheap way to construct a stage is by finding two identical pallets and then covering them with decking as the two photos overleaf show.

The bookshelf in the photo below was acquired from a recycling website and is covered with a tarpaulin at night. There are a variety of instruments – percussion and tuned, but not too many. The children know that although they can transport some resources around the areas, the instruments are expensive and must be kept in this area. In addition to the items seen in the photo, there is also a battery-powered CD player which can be used on the stage.

'Less is more' is a useful phrase to keep in mind when setting up an environment. Select a few high-quality resources, rather than having too many. In the case of instruments, we have decided that these will not be moved to other areas of the garden. However, other resources, such as fabric and blocks, can be moved to where the children need them. Staff teams need to be absolutely clear and consistent with rules such as this.

Diary extracts: examples of development and learning

WHAT TO LOOK OUT FOR

- Children settle very quickly at the start of the new term.
- Children pursuing projects for long periods.
- Children applying knowledge in different situations.
- More children are able to work in groups without an adult.

Ambitious endeavours in the new creative area

Kayra set about making a set of characters and a box for them to live in. Without any adult help, she designed, drew, cut and sewed – creating exactly what she set out to do. This level of perseverance and ambition is rarely seen in tasks set by adults, but very often seen in child-initiated activity.

In these photos, the watch can be seen on Kayra's wrist. By wearing watches in school, the children are experiencing 'telling the time' in real situations, rather than on a worksheet.

Sample learning journeys (see October chapter for explanation)

Identified Areas For Focus:

General/Parents:
encourage friendships with different chn.

Curriculum:
- non-fiction writing, capital letters and full stops.
- * Subtraction.

Identified Areas For Future Focus:
- developing friendships

Year One Learning Journey For ....Hatun.... Date 18.1.16

Hatun was independently reading 'The Smartest Giant in the Town' in the book corner. (T) asked if she could listen. H said "I don't I can't do it." (T) praised her. Hatun read really well. (T) supported her to read some tricky words like 'very and 'already'.

Hatun helped (T) make tricky word bags by finding the right magnetic letters. (T) encouraged her to read each word she was making. She could read was your, said, one, we, all. (T) supported her to read here and where.

Hatun told (T) she had brought her own watch to school. (T) encouraged H to check the time, "11 o'clock" she said. Next step: half past.

Hatun wanted to make ice lollies. (T) encouraged her to think of something healthy. Hatun looked on iPad for fruit smoothies because "you should have 5 a day", she said. (T) asked Hatun where she should search for info. H clicked on the cbbies bar. (T) encouraged H to read a recipe - she decided what ingredients she would need. (T) supported her to read bracket parts. H completed her plan. (T) encouraged her to use capital letters and full stops.

Hatun wanted to make ice lollies. (T) encouraged her to select her ingredients from the food trolley. Hatun looked at her plan and picked things that she needs. (T) modelled how to use a sharp knife. Hatun cut the strawberry and banana. She measured out the milk. (T) helped her to use the blender.

Hatun lay coins on the table (T) asked if she knew how much each one was. Hatun recognised all coins. (T) asked to find £1.00 a prediction then asked to find a different way of making £1.00 using different coins. Hatun found this tricky (T) supported by counting in 10's. Hatun eventually understood.

Hatun was at maths well. She emptied cubes onto the floor and was counting each one as she put them back into the tray. She then placed a few on the table. H said she likes adding but taking away is hard. (T) explained a simpler way to do this using a few cubes @ H found it difficult. (T) provided 100 square for H to understand. eventually H was able to work out using cubes & 100 square.

Hatun was skipping outside. (T) challenged her to see how many she could do. H was skilled at skipping. (T) encouraged her to by counting backwards from 100. H found 100-90 easy. (T) supported her to cross 10 to 89 and again with 79.

Hatun was exploring solids turning into liquids. Hatun made a prediction that it will go slushy after a while when it come out of the fridge it was solid. Hatun eventually understood.

Hatun was exploring monkey dance in P.E. (T) encouraged her to work with someone different. H worked well with her partner. She orally explained their dance sequence. (T) encouraged her to travel like a monkey. She showed the class 3 parts of her sequence.

Identified Areas For Focus:
General/Parents:
Think about what she is learning.
Curriculum:
• Observational drawings.
• Re read written work to check for errors.

Identified Areas For Future Focus:
Time - half past.
Use punctuation marks.

Year One Learning Journey For **Hannah** Date **11.1.16**

PSCHE, RE
I imagine: - Literacy, DT, art & design, music, PE
I understand: - Numeracy, science, history, geography, computing,
Consultation Meeting

Hannah saw her friend m... a puppet

Hannah looked at her focus week watch. Its 20.10 Ⓣ modelled how to read hands explaining the difference between the hour hand and minute hands. Ⓣ explained O'clock, half past, quarter two and quarter past. Ⓣ encouraged her to play whats the time Mr Wolf. Ⓣ supported Hannah to read the times. (She is now confident with O'clock.)

Hannah wanted to paint clay design. Ⓣ showed how to mix colours to make green and pink.

Hannah looked at art book and chose an image she liked. Ⓣ asked questions whilst reading. Hannah discussed what she liked and did not. Ⓣ encouraged to draw from chosen image and showed how to use oil pastels. Hannah commented on 'sunny' colours and looked carefully.

She asked if she could make one. Ⓣ encouraged her to draw her design and wrote the equipment she wanted to use. Ⓣ modelled how to thread a needle and sew a running stitch.

Hannah commented on the weather in morning 'its snowing'. Ⓣ encouraged ho to think about what season we were in. She looked through a weather book and wanted to make a water catcher. Ⓣ explained that you measure weather in m... Ⓣ encouraged Hannah to make predictions.

Hannah was exercising with friends. Ⓣ explained what a pulse was and demonstrated how to feel it. Ⓣ suggested measuring pulse and timed. Hannah recorded her and friends pulses before and after exercise. Hannah spoke about the beat being faster and the numbers getting bigger. Ⓣ got pedometre and explained what it did. Hannah recorded how many steps she did in the day.

Hannah wanted to write a story. She filled out the two planning sheets. Ⓣ Reminded Hannah of the five checks when writing. ① think the sentence. ② Capital letter ③ finger spaces. ④ full stops ⑤ Check what you have written ⑥ Had to remind Hannah throughout to do step 2 and 3. Ⓣ showed Hannah how

to write tricky word were.

Volcanoes continue to interest many of the children and this group set about making a volcano with the clay. They were keen to have a crater in the centre and referred to iPads and books to ensure the accuracy of their design. The co-operation amongst the group was satisfying to witness – these children view their learning as a joyful, shared experience, NOT a competition or a race.

Once decorated, the group were able to make the volcano 'erupt' using ideas from one of the science books in the classroom.

The items in the creative areas continue to be priced and although the daily allowance has risen to 20p per child, Hannah still spent most of her money buying the resources to make this 'alien'.

The waistcoat that Hannah is wearing is to indicate that she was one of the class monitors on this day (see page 101).

The sewing remains popular and the projects are getting more and more ambitious as the pencil case at the beginning of this chapter illustrates. As with all activities, the children complete a design sheet before they begin a project and then they review it afterwards. The concentration and effort are evident in this photo – our main measure of quality.

There are various art books in the creative area and this group became interested in the work of Andy Warhol. They decided to make their own piece of art using photos of themselves which they took to the office to photocopy before they added colour.

Other interesting events

The story scribing and acting is as popular as ever, but very often now the writing is being completed independently, as seen in this example.

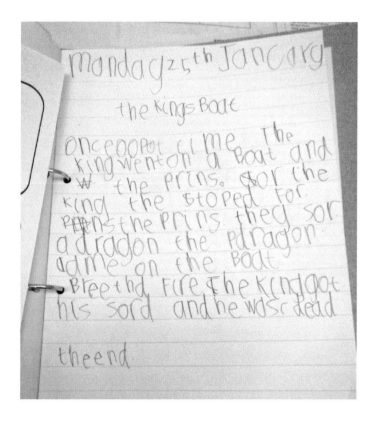

The watches have sparked an interest in telling the time and the game of 'What's the time Mr Wolf?' has been introduced by the staff to engage yet more children. This group are using the clock to indicate the time and including this as a new feature in the traditional game.

In the photo below a group can be seen as they have just completed building this structure. This is not the first time they have done this – it has become a challenge that they enjoy regularly. Each time the structure is slightly different, or has different additions, or is done in a quicker time. The children are challenging themselves within an activity that is familiar.

If you look at the top of this photo, you can see a clock with Numicon around it – an idea from some colleagues in Birmingham.

Part of the curriculum in Year One includes an understanding of past events and how things were different in earlier times. The most relevant of this 'history' work surrounds the children themselves and their own life stories. My previous book *The Nursery Year in Action* details the nursery class in the year 2013–2014 when the cohort of children appearing in this book were in nursery. There are several copies of the nursery book in school and today the children started to look in detail at some of the pictures, pointing out how different some of the children appeared two years' ago!

This final series of pictures from indoors shows once more how children will challenge themselves, given the appropriate resources and environment. Again the emotional environment is key – these children are willing to try new things, safe in the knowledge that their efforts will be recognised and support given if needed. Thus Natasia began to investigate multiplication – the pictures tell the story and although no adult appears in the photos, an adult did step in at two points – on each occasion to offer a resource that would support the learning in a meaningful way.

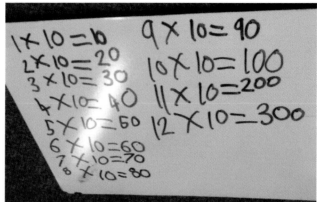

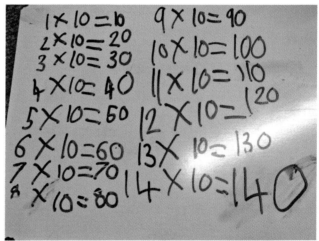

Natasia needed many things to be in place in order for this leap in her learning to have happened. She needed a long period of **time**. She needed enough **space** where no one would spoil what she was doing, **appropriate resources and enough resources**, a **positive, 'can-do' attitude** and an **available adult**. All these things are essential to support the learning of young children.

Equally interesting outdoors!

The sandpit became a long-jump pit today and physical development combined with mathematical awareness as the children used metre sticks to measure and compare the jumps.

 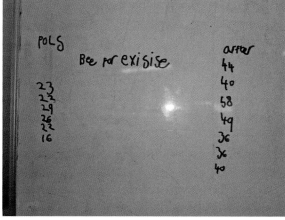

After running around, the children were commenting that they were 'puffed'. Alice encouraged them to check their pulse too and the children began to link the idea of exercise to an increased heart rate. Some concerns were addressed as the group discussed and experimented, gaining information from the adults, each other and the internet. They also recorded the changes before and after exercising.

The photo seen here is a wonderful illustration of teacher impact. If you look back at the October chapter, you can see the photo of Rachel teaching the children how to use the capacity containers to measure the amount of water. This photo is almost identical, as is the conversation, but this time there is no adult present. The children have remembered a previous experience and are now applying the knowledge independently.

This group persevered with this activty for over half an hour. They were deeply involved but chatting and discussing throughout the process. Discussions revolved around shapes, numbers, colours, chalk dust, rain, wind, pressure, floor coverage and time. For me, the most important aspect of this event is that the group were able to negotiate and co-operate without adult support. This emotional resilience may not be assessed in the national curriculum but it is directly linked to how well these children will do in all subjects.

This group have discovered that there are plenty of worms in the mud pit. They have also discovered that the chickens love to eat the worms! Food chain learning in action!

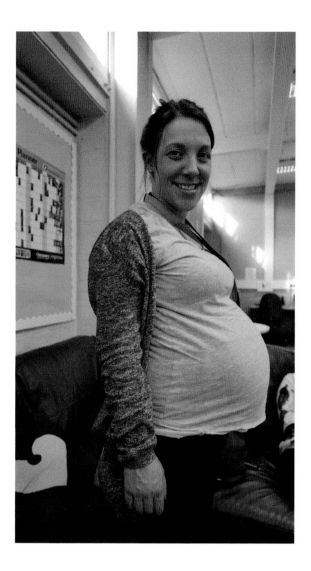

The biggest event for Year One in January 2016 was that Ruth went on maternity leave! She has worked relentlessly to help make Year One a success and is now at home with her daughter, being a brilliant mum!

As January comes to an end, the confidence and independence of the children is striking. They continue to surprise us every day with their ideas and enthusiasm. We are also seeing children pursuing activities for a whole day or longer. The word 'mastery' is being used in education in England at this time and our children are certainly demonstrating mastery within their chosen pursuits. They have the time, space, resources and support to allow them to take their learning to great depth, breadth and complexity. We are only halfway through the year but already the learning has been outstanding. Very excited to see what the rest of the year will bring.

In this chapter I will explain how the routine of the day was changed as a result of staffing issues within the school. Although we are aiming for our 'utopia', we are part of a school and do have to work to fit in with everyone else as well. Thus we have had to compromise with our timetable as I will explain. One other subject discussed in the organisation section is the role of the adult. Although this is mentioned throughout the book, it is worth referring to this aspect of our organisation again. Also in the organisation section, I will look at part of the science curriculum and demonstrate how this is being covered. In the environment section, I will look at the science area within Rhino class and will also look at the science resourcing outdoors, as well as the water area. The diary section will give some examples of the learning that has happened within these areas.

TO DO LIST

- Continue with second cycle of focus children.
- Continue with second cycle of parent meetings.
- Review curriculum coverage at this halfway point.
- Enjoy the half term holiday!
- Celebrate the successes so far this year.

Organisation

Timetable changes

The timetable set out in the September chapter has been working successfully and it suits the children in Year One. However, the school is finding it very difficult to have enough adults available for the maths sessions and therefore it has been agreed to move these sessions to 9.30am – i.e. immediately after the reading sessions. This is far from ideal as it means that the children are in 'adult-directed', sedate sessions for nearly an hour. However, it does mean that once these sessions are complete the rest of the morning can be very flexible. Another event that has impacted on Year One this month has been the beginning of the swimming sessions for two of the classes. Each class will get eight swimming sessions with the first two classes beginning their lessons in February. This means that they have one morning when they are not in school. This has been a big financial commitment from the school, but the benefits are huge.

Because the children are so young, the staff all have to go in the water to help! Several parents also volunteered and they go in the water each week too. Quite a commitment from everyone!

Thus the new timetable looks like this:

8.50 – 9.25	9.25 – 10.00	10.00 – 12.00	12.00 – 12.15	1.25 – 1.40	1.40 – 2.50	2.50 – 3.15
Self-register Group reading and handwriting	Maths input in groups	Free-flow Tidy up	Whole-class group time	Phonics input	Free-flow Tidy up	Whole-class group time

The role of the adult

When moving to a more child-led curriculum, with child-initiated learning occurring for a large portion of each day, many adults become anxious about their role. When training, I have many adults who worry that they will be redundant, since they believe that 'child-initiated learning' means 'let the children get on with the learning on their own'. This is not the case. **While the children are playing, they are learning and the adults are teaching**. Thus the adult role is critical. It is different to the role of an adult in a formal, adult-led setup, and requires many attributes from the adults. The adults in our child-led Year One classes have the following attributes: empathy, flexibility, knowledge of child development, humility, humour, enthusiasm, resourcefulness, organisational skills, practical skills and knowledge of the curriculum. I should stress that when I work in other settings, once the changes have been made and the children are busy, the adults' anxiety disappears as their role becomes clear and they realise just how important they are. I would also stress that in no way is this an easy option. Indeed, it is far easier to sit all the children down, give them a task and then monitor them as they do the set task. It is far more exhausting and demanding to organise an environment and timetable that allows for every child to be catered for as an individual. It is also far more rewarding and enjoyable.

> Teaching should not be taken to imply a 'top down' or formal way of working. It is a broad term which covers the many different ways in which adults help young children learn. It includes their interactions with children during planned and child-initiated play and activities: communicating and modelling language, showing, explaining, demonstrating, exploring ideas, encouraging, questioning, recalling, providing a narrative for what they are doing, facilitating and setting challenges.

This is the Ofsted definition of teaching that I quoted earlier. In the photo opposite, Charlene is interacting with Maria about guinea pigs. During a ten-minute period, Charlene taught in numerous different ways – giving Maria some new vocabulary, showing and explaining how to use an index in a non-fiction book, encouraging her (and also challenging her) to add details to her drawing and facilitating by demonstrating how to draw something (rather than drawing it for her). However, while interacting with Maria, Charlene was also **scanning** the room and this is a vital role that all the adults have to do at all times. Scanning means keeping an eye, an ear and a sixth sense alert for anything that might need attention within the room (or garden). In order to scan effectively the adults have learnt to position themselves at the edge of the area with their back to the outer edge of the area. In this way, they maximise their view of the area.

They will scan for many things:

- Teachable moments. This is the biggest task. As soon as one interaction is completed, the adults will look for the next teachable moment where they can make a difference.
- 'Wow!' moments. When they notice a child doing something independently, for the first time, they will make a note of this to go in the child's file. In many schools the 'Wow!' moments are often duplicated because the staff are unsure if the moment is truly noteworthy. When working in a child-led way, the adults know the children in great detail and they know when something is worth noting.
- Children who are not engaged. Again the adult will observe and then decide what to do. Sometimes children will finish one activity and then there will be a period of 'down time' before they become engaged again. Some children, however, might need a little support – suggestions, challenges, reminders – in order to get involved in something.
- Disputes. As above, the adults will observe disputes in the hope that the children have the skills they need to resolve these themselves. However, they also know individual children very well and will be ready to move if necessary. The children concerned might need reminding about how to resolve the disputes themselves.
- Behaviour. The children know the expectations but occasional reminders are sometimes needed. So, for example, if a child leaves an area without tidying up, then a gentle reminder will be given.
- Resources. If stock runs low or if a different resource is needed, the adult will decide how to respond – either sorting this immediately or making a note and sorting it at the end of the session, or perhaps encouraging the children to write a note to someone in school who might be able to help. I get lots of notes pushed under my door requesting all sorts of items.
- Potential dangers (trip hazards, children doing something dangerous, etc.) The adult will then decide whether they need to move to resolve the danger, or if a child can be directed to sort this out.
- Noise levels indoors. As stated, we expect children to use quiet voices indoors – and again gentle reminders might be needed.

'Multi-tasking' is an essential skill for anyone working in a child-led setting. Each adult will be interacting and involved with an individual or group of children, but they are constantly scanning and aware of the needs of the whole group. They are alert and ready to move if needed. When assessing our adults, we use levels of involvement on them too. Our adults are expected to be at level 5 involvement – interacting with the children. In child-initiated learning the adults are critical and they cannot be chatting to each other, nor can they be indifferent to events. They are each a vital part of the process – whatever their pay scale. We do not have a rota for the staff – they work as a team and will go where they are needed. Thus if all children are outdoors, they will all go out. The hierarchy is far less obvious than in more formal settings. The support staff interact and teach, just as the teachers do. The teachers have overall responsibility for the assessment and tracking of the children. They also plan the maths, reading and phonic sessions but any observer of a session would not be able to tell who are the teachers and who are the support staff.

Curriculum coverage

Curriculum 'coverage' is a huge source of stress for teachers in England. I am often questioned about how we ensure that every child accesses all subjects and the whole curriculum. The same concern is raised in our early years classes as well. However, the staff are monitoring individual children and they know who has accessed what. If gaps are found, then we will amend the environment and resources to ensure the children are attracted to pursue play that will 'fill the gap'. Indeed, our staff are much more confident about this than staff in schools where there is a very formal 'whole class' teaching model. Adults from very formal settings describe to me how they spend their time doing maths and literacy focus tasks and they are able to say what the children can do within the narrow parameters of the tasks. However, they report that they do not know the 'whole child', they do not understand the different and unique characteristics of learning that each child demonstrates and they do not therefore know how best to teach them. They try, and fail, to make every child learn the same things in the same way. They report how stressful and upsetting it is for the staff and the children. Many people believe that whole class teaching is the best way to ensure coverage but what exactly does 'coverage' mean? We can sit the children down and tell them about the lifecycle of a frog; they can even complete a worksheet. We can then say we have covered that aspect of the curriculum but we don't know how much each child has learnt unless we spend time 'testing' them. When working in a more child-led way, the children are constantly demonstrating their knowledge and understanding without the need for testing. The adults spend their time interacting with the children, constantly observing and interpreting what their observations tell them. The best education is one that teaches children **how to learn**. Content-driven education systems teach children to do as they are told. (It is no coincidence that the current government supports such a system.) We are trying to teach our children in Year One how to learn, but we are doing this through whatever interests them, recognising that they are all unique, interested in different things and equipped with different approaches to learning.

If we take one aspect of the science curriculum, we can demonstrate how the coverage looks in practice.

Animals, including humans

	Environment	Example 1	Example 2
I can spot and name a variety of common animals.	In school there are real fish, rabbits, chickens, guinea pigs, pond animals. There are sets of realistic plastic animals in the classrooms, many books and access to the internet for research.	Children went to the pet shop to buy the guinea pigs. While they were there they saw many other animals.	The children sort the toy animals into the correct groups – according to their 'habitats' on the shelving. (See photo overleaf.)
I can spot and name a variety of common animals that are carnivores, herbivores and omnivores.	The children are responsible for feeding the fish, chickens, rabbits, guinea pigs and pond creatures.	The children dig up worms and feed them to the chickens.	The children read the guinea pig books carefully to decide what to feed them.
I can describe and compare the structure of a variety of common animals (fish, amphibians, reptiles, birds and mammals, including pets).	The animals in the environment cover all these varieties except reptiles. We also have magnifying glasses, bug boxes, reference books, plastic animals.	Children found newts in the pond and thought they were baby alligators. This led to discussions and investigations.	Children find a long worm and say 'It's a snake'. Adults interact to extend the discussion. 'Is a worm a reptile?' (Now that's got you thinking!)
I can name, draw and label the basic parts of the human body and say which part of the body is to do with each sense.	Skeleton, human body puzzles, stethoscope, books, plants, flowers, cooking opportunities, **children and adults!**	Adults interact with children as they cook – encouraging them to look, smell and taste new foods.	Children notice the smell of burning when the cakes are overdone!

We have looked at every statement in the curriculum to ensure that our environment offers the best possible opportunities for coverage. In addition, our maths, reading and phonic sessions ensure we have 'covered' the literacy and maths content, but, as stated before, we want the children to apply these skills in areas that interest them. We know that the interest will deliver engagement and then the children will challenge and push themselves further than if we dictate the content.

Setting up the environment

Specialist science area indoors

As explained earlier, each classroom now has a 'specialism' and Rhino class now has a lot of the science resources for the year group. In the October chapter, I described the cooking resources and, of course, **cooking involves numerous subjects** – literacy (reading and writing recipes and methods), maths (weighing and measuring quantities and sizes), art and design (designing the look of the final product) and **science** (changing states of materials, combining materials, heat, cold, temperature, etc.). It can also involve history (recipes from the past), geography (recipes from other countries), RE (special food associated with festivals, etc.). The most powerful learning is not subject driven, it is the learning that is driven by the child's interest and cooking is a superb example of this. In the December chapter I described some of the art and creative areas and resources. Here again the resources lend themselves to cross-curricular

learning including **science** – clay, sewing, collage work, all involve consideration and discussion about materials and their properties. But back to the 'science' area in Rhino class. There are two open shelving units containing numerous items that the children might need. They are stored, either directly on the shelves or in low open trays, allowing easy access and visibility. We still have several children who are in the early stages of learning English and this way of storing resources allows them to be as independent as possible. Resources available include:

- reference books and some 'science experiment' books (so that the children can select their own experiments to do), puzzles, magnetic resources and labels;
- planning sheets (see Appendix K) – to encourage hypothesising, prediction, planning and review (these sheets are either completed independently or as a shared process with an adult, as appropriate);
- electricity equipment – batteries, wires, crocodile clips, bulbs, buzzers;
- various substances – bicarbonate of soda, corn flour, oil, soap powder, salt, food colouring, washing up liquid, lemon juice – and these can be added to if children request an item;
- timers, stop watches, tape measures, rulers, metre sticks, scales (various types);
- Bee-Bots;
- light box and visualiser;
- microscope, magnifying glasses, binoculars, etc.;
- syringes, pipettes, measuring cylinders, jugs, etc.;
- mixing bowls, trays, funnels, containers of various sizes.

The two photos on the next page show the area in use. The children have decided what they are going to do – either as a result of a question, a conversation, an event, or from looking in one of the books – they have completed a planning sheet (which they have paid for!), they have selected the equipment that they need and they are carrying out their task. If they need adult help, they will ask for it but they will often ask their friends first, revelling in the opportunity for independence and challenge.

Science outdoors (including water area)

As soon as the children step outdoors, they are in a scientific environment because they are exposed to **the weather and the seasons**. They experience the leaves blowing off the trees in Autumn, the frozen puddles in Winter, the daffodils in Spring (although as mentioned before these did flower in December last year!) and the heat of Summer. They see and feel what the force of the wind can do, how the rain gathers in gutters and drips to the ground, how the sand behaves differently according to whether there has been rain or not, etc. Of course the **adults** are the ever-present resource which is critical to add the language, vocabulary, ponderings and suggestions to these situations – **capitalising on every learning opportunity** that they can.

In addition to the weather and seasons there are the following areas to enhance scientific enquiry which have been dealt with in other chapters:

- woodwork area (see November chapter for details) – relevant to materials, forces, scientific enquiry;
- stage and music area (see January chapter) – relevant to senses;
- sand area (see October chapter) – relevant to materials, forces, weather, seasons, rivers, mountains, etc.;
- physical equipment (see December chapter) – relevant to body parts and function, forces, speed, direction, scientific enquiry;
- snack area (see March chapter) – relevant to animal groups and human senses.

In addition to all the above, we have the following:

- **Animals** – chickens, rabbits, guinea pigs, pond-life and mini-beasts. There are also fish indoors.

The rabbits and chickens are in large purpose-built enclosures, within which there are hutches. The children are responsible for feeding and cleaning out the animals.

- **The pond** – This was built by the children (see September chapter) and five months on it contains various forms of life for the children to investigate and study. The children have placed logs around the pond and have magnifying glasses and books nearby to use as they wish.

- **Mini-beast area** – We have one small area of grass in the outdoor environment and there are bushes, logs and rocks to encourage mini-beasts (and therefore birds) to visit. There is some natural shelving with books, magnifying glasses, bug boxes, binoculars, etc. to support the children's investigations.

- **Growing area** – With the chickens often out and about in the outdoor area, growing fruit and vegetable plants is proving even more challenging than normal. The two boys in the photo opposite are showing the chickens their 'scarecrow' which they are going to place on the fence of the growing area in an attempt to scare the chickens away. The children are, however, seeing the processes involved in growing food and the challenges that need to be overcome. The area includes a compost bin, into which the children put the waste from their snacks and from cleaning out the animals, as well as some of the leftovers from lunch.

- **Digging area** – This is basically a large pit of mud and the area is used in many ways. The mud is used for various role play adventures – including potions, recipes, combining with water and other items, building dams, volcanoes, etc. In fact it is used in very similar ways to the sand but behaves differently and appeals to different groups of children. Scientific enquiry pervades the play – e.g. changing states of materials, discussions about volcanoes, dams, beavers, habitats, solids, liquids, etc. The mud also delivers many mini-beasts which again leads into scientific enquiry and discussion. A recent activity (as mentioned in the January chapter) has been digging up worms to feed to the chickens – discussions about lifecycles, omnivores, herbivores and carnivores then ensue.

Water investigation area

The children in Year One are aged five and six and they love to play with water. Indeed, children of all ages enjoy water and it is a wonderful vehicle for scientific learning and learning in all subjects. Some of the resources on offer are different to those in nursery or Reception. For example, the containers are **measuring containers** with markings to indicate quantities of liquid in millilitres, etc. We have also purchased a large quantity of **drain pipes and connectors**. The pipes have been cut to specific lengths – half metre, metre, two metre, etc. and the measurements have been written on the pipes with permanent marker. The connectors are simple 'push joints' so that the children can create long routes for the water to travel. There are also large pieces of **guttering, Creative Cascade stands, trays at various heights, flexible hoses, funnels, syringes** and **pipettes** for further investigation.

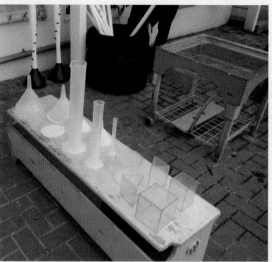

Diary extracts: examples of development and learning

WHAT TO LOOK OUT FOR

- Children cover many 'subjects' of the curriculum within one project.
- Overall curriculum coverage is good and any gaps have been addressed.
- Children remain independent and confident – still keen to learn and to challenge themselves.
- Many boys seem to suddenly make a leap in their development.

The human body

A group of girls start to role play paramedics and are attempting CPR on each other. An adult steps in and explains that this can be very dangerous, describing the organs within the body that can be damaged by this game. She then reminds the group about the books they can use to find out more information and also about the magnetic body and body-part labels. The group become engrossed reading the books and then complete the puzzle accurately.

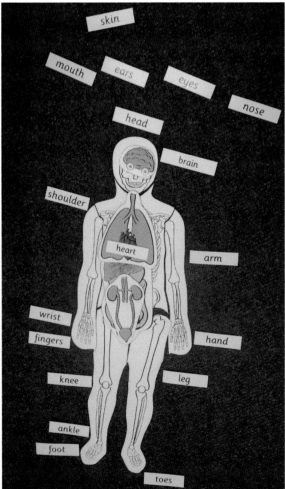

Sample learning journeys (see October chapter for explanation)

Identified Areas For Focus:
General/Parents:
Curriculum:
• story writing - full stops
• read letters
• Time
• Money
Identified Areas For Future Focus:
• Science experiment
• encourage other
friendship group

Year One Learning Journey For Sianna Rose **Date** 22.7.16

Sianna-Rose wanted to make doughnuts with a group of friends. Ⓣ helped the group search the internet for a recipe. Ⓣ Read the ingredients and the method. Sianna-Rose wrote it down by herself. Ⓣ Kept reminding Sianna-Rose to add finger space and capital letters at the start of a sentence. Ⓣ emphasis some of the sounds so that Sianna-Rose can write the words herself. Ⓣ helped Sianna-Rose use the kilogram scale. Sianne-Rose measured out the sugar and the butter. Sianna-Rose left the dough to rise. Ⓣ explains how the yeast is helping it to fermentate the dough. Sianna-Rose made it into small balls and put her finger in it to make the wholes in the doughnut. Ⓣ fry the doughnuts in the oil. Ⓣ encouraged her to evaluate the doughnuts. Sianna-Rose just wrote one word. Ⓣ helped her to extend her sentence.

PSCHE, RE
I imagine: - Literacy, D&T, art & design, music, PE
I understand: - Numeracy, science, history, geography, computing,
Consultation Meeting

Sianna-Rose told T about what she did during the holidays. T suggested to write about it. T introduced a story plan, talked about the beginning, the middle, the end. T supported Sianna by reminding her of the diagraphs. T also talked about present and past. T encourage S to write her story in the past tense explaining that it is because it already happened. S wrote her story independently.

Sianna-Rose took a science sheet. Ⓣ encouraged sianna to use the 10p for the change. Sianna Rose was not sure how much money she had. Ⓣ counted with sianna Rose. Sianna-Rose kept counting the 2p as one penny. Ⓣ modelled counting. Ⓣ then showed Sianna-Rose different change. Ⓣ Also explained to Sianna-Rose how she can put a number in her head and count the rest on her fingers. Sianna-Rose listened and was doing sums using the coins. Sianna-Rose was counting in two's with the two penny's. Ⓣ Praised Sianna-Rose for listening and doing the sums independently.

Sianna-Rose was able to do a variety of different patch balances in P.E. She successfully did one on her stomach. Ⓣ encouraged her to hold it.

Sianna-Rose shows Ⓣ her watch. Ⓣ what time is it? Sianna Rose is not sure. Ⓣ Explains the minute hand and the hour hand. Ⓣ also explains half past and quarter past to Sianna-Rose. Sianna-Rose "11 gone 5" Ⓣ models language "5 past 11 you mean". Sianna-Rose comes back after and says Now "It is 10 past 12". Ⓣ Praise Sianna-Rose for remembering her time. Sianna-Rose remembers O'clock as well.

the science. Sianna-Rose looks through the book and wants to do a yeast experiment. Ⓣ encourage Sianna-Rose to make a prediction. Sianna-Rose made a prediction and wrote the equipment and the method. Ⓣ helped sianna-Rose to measure out the ingredients and make the milk frothy. Ⓣ explains why we had to leave the dough to rise. After two hours Sianna-Rose and friend seen that there was lot of bubbles in the dough and it has rised and incresed in size. Sianna-Rose "It's really sticky". "It has lots of bubbles." Ⓣ explain the fermentation of the bread. After baking the bread. Ⓣ encourage S to evaluate and make a conclusion.

Identified Areas For Focus:
General/Parents:

Curriculum:
* Story writing - Extend
* Sentences, punctuation
* Intro. simple mult.

Identified Areas For Future Focus:
* Geography
* Time
* Physical - team games

Year One Learning Journey For **Harley**   Date **29.2.16**

PSCHE, RE
I imagine: - Literacy, D&T, art & design, music, PE
I understand: - Numeracy, science, history, geography, computing,
Consultation Meeting

Harley was playing with the toy animals. She wondered which country the animals came from. (T) helped her to look for a picture of the animal on the globe. Harley found a picture of a lion. (T) asked her which country it was & explained that it was Africa. Harley Her found Africa herself on the globe.

After playing with the animals, H wanted to write a story about a lion, she chose characters to use + included the model she had made out of blocks in the morning. (T) reminded her about using the story plan. H got the globe to find how to write 'Africa'. (T) encouraged H to talk about what was going to happen in her story & how what is.

Harley looks through the science book. Marley wants to make bread which is the yeast experiment. (T) encouraged Harley to write the prediction, method, equipment and the method. Harley wrote it independently. (T) talks about why we have to leave the dough on a hot radiator for a while. After some time, Harley "look at the dough". (T) explains how the yeast has helped the dough to fermentate. (T) shows the bubbles that have formed. (T) helps the girls to knead and put it in a loaf shape. Bakes the dough. After making the bread Harley taste it. (T) supports Harley to write the conclusion and the evaluation. (T) Praise Harley for extending her sentences.

Harley wanted to write her story using her plan. (T) encouraged H to think of a title & then gave H some suggestions for an opener. H was able to write independently. (T) suggested making her writing more interesting by using adjectives. (T) explained what they were & gave H some examples. H chose some to use in her story. H used some speech in her story. (T) explained about speech marks & showed H how to use them. H then used them in more speech. When H was unsure of a couple of tricky words (T) reminded her to use words around her. H was able to find and copy words. Once H had written her story she acted it out with her friends.

Harley was using the iPad. (T) noticed she found addition very easy & asked Harley to try multiplication. Harley "What that"? (T) explains the different signs eg add, take away & multiply. Harley said "It looks to hard". (T) encouraged H to use the numicon to work out her answers. & showed her a strategy to use. H found it tricky to begin with but eventually managed to work out the answers independently and was proud to show her peers what she had learnt.

Harley was encouraged by a group of friend to play Hockey. H was a bit unsure. T explained the rules. H had a go at playing. I praise

Harley shows her watch. (T) ask her the time. Harley confident in saying the O'clock. (T) encouraged her to think about the half past and quarter past. (T) kept reminding her during the day. the half past and quarter past

Grouping animals

Every time the toy animals are used, they have to be returned to the shelves and every time this happens there are discussions about where they should go, comments such as 'No, that one lives in the sea', 'I think this one eats meat too', 'Is this a reptile?'. The books nearby are often referred to for answers to questions, but the children know who to ask in the year group – they know which children are the experts. For these children their interest in animals means that they retain the knowledge that they hear and they can explain it to others. For me the most powerful message here is that these children are learning how to learn – they realise that each child has their own set of talents and they are all valued. They are learning to learn from each other and by themselves – in no way do they see the adults as the only 'teachers'.

Non-fiction books

The photo here shows Rachel reading a non-fiction book to a small group who are interested. Indeed, the non-fiction books have become increasingly popular and children have started to make their own. In the photo opposite, we see the children sharing their non-fiction books with the class at the end of the day. They are all about different subjects – including dolphins (by Skylar) and scuba-diving (by Lee).

The children have relatively short periods of time when they are required to sit and listen. Therefore, when they are on the carpet, they can focus and this photo shows the audience listening carefully to their friends.

In all the classes there are book areas, with fiction and non-fiction books organised and displayed carefully. Again – less is more. If there are too many books, it is difficult for children to see them and to select the one that they want.

Mixtures and potions

The light box, like all other resources, is always available. It is part of the continuous provision – not something that is used just once a year. It is used very regularly and whenever a child is interested.

Every time I go into the Year One classrooms there is an 'experiment' taking place that involves various liquids, food colouring and deep concentration. On this occasion, just before the final ingredient was added, the children asked if they could place the container on the light box. This led to a discussion about the dangers of water coming into contact with electricity. However, not to be deterred, the children found a clear box, placed their 'experiment' in that, placed it on the light box and then added the final ingredient (in this case bicarbonate of soda). They were delighted with the added visual effects. Again an adult was nearby, encouraging the children to look, listen and smell – using all their senses. In this, as with many of the experiments, it is not the outcome or the facts learnt that are important (as these will inevitably be forgotten). What is important is that the children are learning to make predictions, follow instructions, observe carefully and record their findings. They are learning how to hypothesise and 'test' ideas systematically. They are learning that their ideas and opinions are important and valid. They are learning that sometimes their predictions are correct and sometimes not but that, in either case, it is the process that is valuable and rewarding. Gradually they gain knowledge which might help them with their next prediction. As the science curriculum demands – they are learning to work scientifically.

Funky fountain

It's not all complex potions and mixtures either. In the photo above, this group of boys are playing with a simple toy (a funky fountain) which is basically a pipe with holes in it. The boys pour water into the pipe and the stoppers can be opened or closed. Some of these boys played with the same toy in nursery; the level of involvement was equally high, but the learning was very different. In nursery, they were learning new vocabulary to do with the toy and water, to share the space, to take turns opening the stoppers (in a random order) and to pour the water in the pipe (rather than all over the floor). They were squealing when they got wet and then repeating the game over again. In Year One, the same piece of equipment delivers very different learning. There are questions, predictions, tests and observations. Through this they learn, for example, that the water shoots out further when the pipe is full but only one stopper is opened, that one container of water reaches to the second bung, that it takes about ten seconds for all the water to empty if all the bungs are opened at once, etc. They are playing scientifically, they are deeply involved, new synapses are forming. Active, powerful learning is happening.

Clay – art or science or geography or RE or maths or literacy or history?

The clay is used for many projects – for example, for Fideline to make a mermaid. As a potter in my spare time, I am drawn to such activity and can offer advice and suggestions. In this case, I noticed how much water the children were adding to the clay. I explained that this would weaken their models and together we pondered how they could rectify the situation. Paper towels did the job well. I was then able to model how to make 'slip' which can be used as 'glue' to join pieces of clay together without weakening the finished model. Fideline is fascinated by mermaids and, because she is able to pursue her own interests, she brings this theme to many areas. The photos below show one of her clay models and one made at the woodwork bench. She also wrote stories featuring these characters.

Electricity

The science planning sheets can be seen in the next two photos.

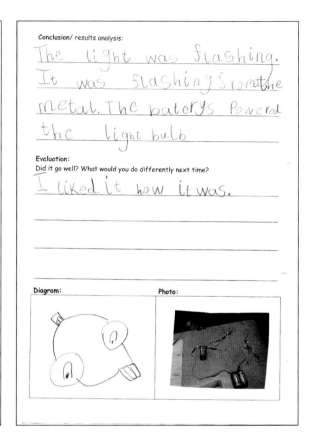

Experiment

Name: _____ Date: 14.1.16

I will be testing Electric

Prediction:

It will make it light up with the electric

Equipment:
1: Lights	6:
2: cables	7:
3: Baterys	8:
4:	9:
5:	10:

Method:
1: clip the cable on the light.
2: Put the baterys on the cable
3: Put another cable on
4:
5:
6:
7:

Conclusion/ results analysis:

The light was flashing. It was flashing from the metal. The baterys Powerd the light bulb

Evaluation:
Did it go well? What would you do differently next time?

I liked it how it was.

Diagram: Photo:

Technological toys

Kieran became fascinated by the challenge of creating a toy that would move upwards on strings. He referred to the science books, tried several techniques and eventually succeeded in creating a toy that met his success criteria. This level of challenge probably would not have been set by an adult since the chance of success would have been slim. However, by letting the children select their own activity, they constantly surprise us with the levels they strive to reach.

The science of sound

Cinar was equally determined in his efforts to make some musical pipes using straws. Both books and the iPad were used for reference and the discussions revolved around how the length of pipe would alter the sound it made. As with many such events, once one child had made an instrument, others wanted to become involved. Cinar then became the expert, teaching other children and, in doing so, reinforcing his own understanding.

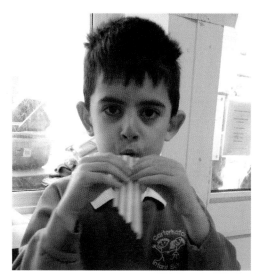 

Bee–Bot challenge

The Bee-Bots continue to be popular, but with this resource too, the 'mastery' is becoming evident. The children are no longer satisfied with the basic manoeuvres. The photos below show how they are measuring how far one unit of movement will be and then creating pathways using the blocks for the Bee-Bot to travel through.

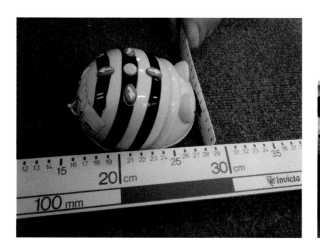 

Ice

An old chocolate box reminded this group of an ice cube maker and so they set about making their own ice cubes. Once frozen, the children discussed how long the ice cubes would take to melt. Abdirahman 'hypothesised' that they would melt more quickly if he held one in his hand because his hand was warm. Someone else thought that the radiator would be even warmer. Rachel encouraged the children to write down their predictions for the melting times and the children were keen to do this.

 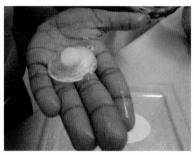 

Through these few examples, I hope it is clear that when children pursue their own interests, their learning is holistic – covering many subjects, and often including aspects of science. It is the role of the adults to introduce new concepts, vocabulary or skills as appropriate to the situation, without taking over the play from the child. This requires great skill and sound knowledge of each child. However, even when an adult is not involved, the children will learn from each other, from the environment and by pushing themselves to figure something out.

Although a short calendar month and an even shorter school month (because of the half term break), the children continue to demonstrate deep levels of involvement. We are over halfway through the year and feel no need to amend the way we are working. With the backing of SLT, we can continue to the Easter break without having to increase the amount of adult-led sessions. Lucky, lucky children!

7 | March

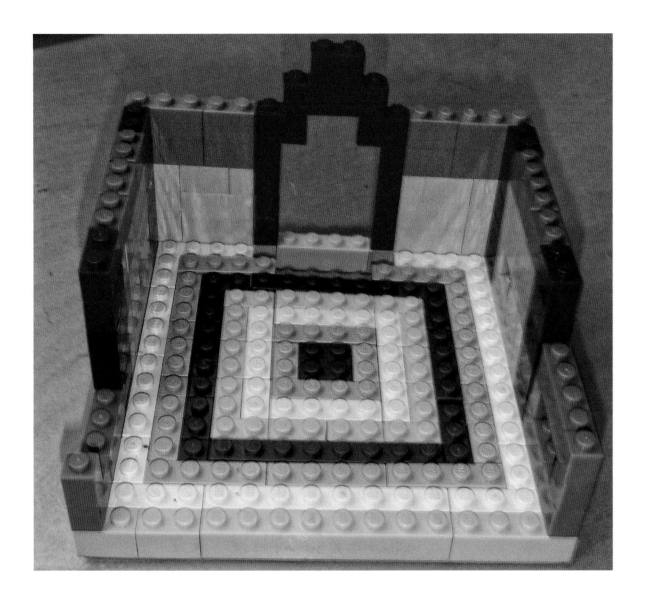

In this chapter I will briefly discuss assessment and moderation, and will also describe the decisions from the review meeting held this term. In the environment section, I will look briefly at the specialism in the third classroom (cooking), as well as the small construction equipment indoors. Outdoors, I will describe the large construction equipment and the snack area. The diary section contains a wide variety of events – with examples to show coverage of all curriculum subjects.

TO DO LIST

- Complete second cycle of focus children.
- Complete second cycle of parent meetings.
- Review curriculum coverage.
- Complete end of term assessments.
- Meet as a year group team and decide on any changes for the Summer Term.

Organisation

Assessments and moderation

As mentioned, as I write this book, England is in a time of change with regards to assessment – often referred to as 'Life after levels' since the children are not now supposed to be tracked by levels such as 2a, 3b, etc. However, every school is trying to find its own way through this confusion, but with the phonics screening test, SATs in Year Two and detailed statutory requirements in the curriculum, there is very little scope to be creative with assessments. We, like many other schools, have purchased an electronic tracking system but, since the whole system is new, it has not been fully trialled and is proving too time-consuming. We are therefore tracking the key indicators for maths and literacy (the statutory statements within the national curriculum) and we are tracking individuals using ongoing teacher assessments for the other subjects. Our teachers meet with a member of the senior leadership team each term and at this meeting they discuss each child in turn. They consider whether each child is making expected or better progress and, if not, they are able to explain what the barriers are and what is being done to overcome any issues. There was little new numerical data at the end of this term but the progress meetings were still full of detail about each child, their unique situation and their progress. In every case, progress was as the teachers expected. For some, this meant huge leaps in attainment. For others the tiny steps of progress were as expected, taking into account the child's additional needs or recognising the impact if there had been trauma in a child's life.

In addition, the teachers met with staff from four other local schools to look, in particular, at the writing levels of the children in Year One. The other schools had a greater 'quantity' of writing from their Year One children, but the vast majority was adult-directed work. However, once the writing from all the schools was scrutinised in detail, to look at levelling, it was agreed that the levels across the schools was very similar. Therefore, although our children had had no adult-directed writing tasks at this point, their attainment was the same as schools where they had far more structured, adult-directed lessons. The group did not discuss the quality of the content, which could have been a very interesting discussion.

Review of timetable and structure of the day

Year One is probably the most challenging year in primary school. Within the year group there are children who are reading and writing fluently and independently, and others who are just becoming confident talkers; there are some who can grasp multiplication and others who are just learning to count accurately up to ten; there are some who can walk on their hands and others who still need encouragement to jump off a low platform; there are some who can organise a large group in a co-operative game and others who are just learning to take turns with resources. The staff are aware of this massive diversity and, until this point, they feel they have met all the needs of the children in the structure that we have organised. At the end of term review meeting, the teachers all agreed that they would like to continue in exactly the same way until the end of the year. However, after a long discussion, some changes were agreed and these are explained in the April chapter. These discussions vary each year, depending on the cohort of children, their development and what this means for the structure of Year Two. Whatever your school situation, it is vital to look at the children to see what will best meet their needs now, rather than where they need to be in two or three years' time.

Setting up the environment

Specialist cooking area

Food for cooking is paid for by the school. Once a fortnight, we place an online order with one of the large supermarkets to ensure that the basics are in stock. If specialist items are needed, then either the children will go to the local shop, or they will write a shopping list and give it to a member of staff so that they can buy the items on their way home.

As explained, the three classes now each have a 'specialist area' and all 90 children can go to whichever class they choose during their free-flow sessions. The Gorilla class now has all the cooking equipment and ingredients. The equipment described in the October chapter is now stored on more permanent shelving in Gorilla class, along with the cookery books, some extra equipment (such as a blender) and design sheets.

Two completed design sheets are shown below.

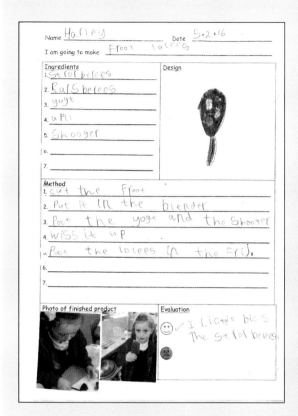

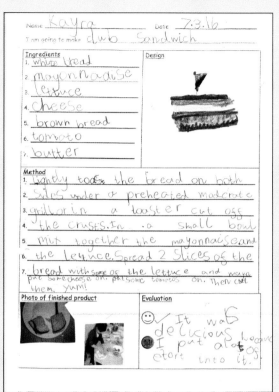

Small construction and 'small world' equipment

Although each class now has a specialism, there are some resources still available in all classes and the small construction and small world equipment is included in this. There are some variations across the three rooms but in selecting the equipment, the same principles have been applied. We are looking for high-quality, open-ended, challenging equipment. The photo at the beginning of this chapter shows what the outcomes can be. The Lego model is quite remarkable in its level of sophistication. This 'mastery' will never be seen in schools where the children have half an hour of 'golden time'

When glancing at this picture, it is easy to overlook the things that need to be in place to facilitate this type of project. These children have physical space and long periods of time in which to play. They are also emotionally safe – confident that no-one will spoil their efforts and that the adults will support them if needed. They have learnt to work together, to persevere and to be creative in order to succeed. They are independent, confident learners.

on a Friday. To work to this level a child needs appropriate resources, enough time, a clear calm space, ambition, perseverance and self-motivation. The unit blocks, from Community Playthings, are also available in each class, as are some wooden train sets, polydrons, k'nex, quality model animals and story characters. The children are free to combine the resources and to add to them (making their own props, scenes, signs, etc.) In the photo below, the Lego has been combined with the story characters, creating a 3D scene for the characters to enter. This then led to a story being scribed, with the visual prompt of the actual scene supporting the narrative, as it helped the child visualise and create the events.

Large construction outdoors

The resources we have selected for outdoors are different to indoors. Outdoors the children can be louder, messier and do 'bigger' things. We have ensured that all subjects are covered both indoors and outdoors, but in different ways. For example, it is really difficult to keep small Lego outdoors as the pieces fall down drains or get buried in the sand. Far better to have large blocks, fabric and tyres outside as these are less likely to get lost and there is more space, which means the scale of the resources can be exploited. In the photo overleaf, the large blocks from Community Playthings can be seen in use. The children have taken them out of the shed and have combined them with some of the other resources available. I am constantly on the lookout for new

The surface in this area was concrete blocks. We have placed sleepers as a boundary and filled the area with bark to a depth of 10cm. This creates a softer surface and changes the atmosphere of an area.

items to add to this area and skips and ditches often provide interesting things to add. Anything that will not be destroyed by the rain is left uncovered (crates, logs, etc.). Other items are put in salt bins, on shelving covered with tarpaulin or in a shed that the children can access themselves.

A good starting kit would include:

Car tyres
Go–kart tyres
Large pieces of fabric (stored in a
    salt bin)
Carpet pieces
Car parts (bumpers, steering wheels,
    booster seats)
Pipes, guttering, hoses, ropes
Crates and bread trays

Smaller wooden blocks
Planks of wood
Cardboard boxes
Pipe insulation
Bamboo canes
Large pegs or grips
Logs

This group persevered for over half an hour to create a ramp, up which they could roll a go-kart tyre at speed, so that it would 'leap' over the crates at the end. They needed a smooth, steep ramp, with barriers at the sides. Eventually they succeeded.

Snack area outdoors

As mentioned, most of the children in Year One have come through our Reception and nursery. They have learnt to 'listen' to their own body – a vital life-skill – to know if they are too hot or cold, to know if they are thirsty and to know if they are hungry. Thus we don't tell the children when to wear their coats in cold weather (although we do insist on them wearing coats if it is raining). We will encourage them to think about how they feel and then decide for themselves. Similarly, with snack time, we do not have a set time for snack or drinks in the early years or in Year One. The children can decide when they need a drink or a snack and these are available in the outdoor area. There is just water to drink and the snack is fruit or salad items funded by the lottery.

The children are responsible for washing the cups and for putting scraps into the compost bin or into the feed bowl for the animals.

Diary extracts: examples of development and learning

WHAT TO LOOK OUT FOR

- Many children make sudden leaps in their development.
- Curriculum coverage remains strong.
- Many activities are cross-curricular with previous learning being applied in new areas.
- Assessments show good or outstanding progress.

The examples in this diary section are all from a couple of weeks in March in Year One. At the end of each entry, I have noted the subjects that were covered. This illustrates how futile it is to divide learning into subjects and also how much easier it is to cover the curriculum via activities such as the ones seen every day in Year One at this time. It should also be noted that in every example the children are displaying the characteristics of effective learning – which have been proven to be strong indicators of future attainment.

Volcanoes

The interest in volcanoes continues and the sand area is an excellent place to build a volcano. The children then wanted the eruption that they had created indoors and eventually this was achieved. (Science, design and technology, history, geography, physical development, numeracy, literacy, PSE.)

Sample learning journeys (see October chapter for explanation)

Identified Areas For Focus:
General/Parents:
Friendships.
Curriculum:
· Stories/Reading
· Geography/history
· DT

Identified Areas For Future Focus:
Use finger spaces.
Continue to read
regularly

Year One Learning Journey For **Rayhan** Date **7.3.16**

PSCHE, RE ✓
I imagine: - Literacy, D&T, art & design, music, PE
I understand: - Numeracy, science, history, geography, computing,
Consultation Meeting

Rayhan read his reading book from home. Rayhan sounded out each word - Ⓣ supported Rayhan with split diagraphs - come, gave. and the charac name. Ⓝ Need to improve sight vocabulary

Rayhan came to say he needed the police (Ⓣ). Ⓣ played along as a police officer and asked questions. Ⓣ encouraged him to make a police report! Rayhan was very excited and got friends to join him. Ⓣ supported to sound out. Ⓣ explained what a header was and encouraged him to use question words, who, what, where and how. Rayhan was very clear about what happened. He then suggested making a microphone. Ⓣ encouraged and in acted an interview with him. Rayhan lost interest in making a microphone but was keen to do a news show with friends. Ⓣ asked details about show, parts and supplied a police outfit. Ⓣ encouraged to make sign. Rayhan and friends made a big sign together taking it in turns to write letters. Rayhan decided on his part as police sergeant and wanted his turn to be interviewed

Rayhan was talking about swimming. Ⓣ asked how we get there - 'coach'. Ⓣ suggested thinking about how to get from the classroom to the coach. Ⓣ modelled left and right, showing the 'L' on your hand can help you remember left. Rayhan walked from classroom to office. Ⓣ stopped at intervals and asked for directions. Rayhan was able to successfully verbalise using left and right. Ⓣ asked him to look through doors and imagine walking to coach. 'We would go left and then go right to get into the coach'. Ⓣ suggested drawing map. Rayhan looked at video of walk filmed by his friend and used his memory to draw an accurate simple map.

Rayhan was making a submarine out of lego. Ⓣ suggested looking at an ipad for photos of old ones. Rayhan looked at the variety of designs and was impressed. Ⓣ explained they were old drawings of submarines because not many of the actual submarines were still about. Rayhan wanted to make a submarine. Ⓣ supported him to fill out design plan. Ⓣ supplied cardboard tube and inquired how he would cut? Rayhan understood a saw would work best. Rayhan chose to cover in foil to 'make it look metal'. Ⓣ encouraged him to make a propeller. Rayhan wanted to put another bit of tube on. Ⓣ showed how a bottle lid would be used. Rayhan liked idea and was happy with product

Rayhan was making with lego. Ⓣ asked what it was and found it was a walkie talkie. Ⓣ introduced lego plan and explained how you can design first. Ⓣ encouraged to complete plan retrospectively as a practice. Rayhan drew, counted bricks and wrote an evaluation.

Identified Areas For Focus:

General/Parents:
develop confidence

Curriculum:
* letter formation a, d, g (curly caterpillar)
* takeaway - finding change about recall

Identified Areas For Future Focus:
Gross and fine motor skills - to support handwriting

PSCHE, RE
I imagine:- Literacy, D&T, art & design, music, RE
I understand:- Numeracy, science, history, geography, computing.
Consultation Meeting

Lee wanted to buy an iped costing 6p "I don't have the money" he said. (T) encouraged L to see what coins he had - '2 10ps, 5p.' (T) encouraged L to choose coin that was more than 6p He chose 1p (T) explained finding change using number bonds 6+ □ =10. Lee knew straight away. (T) encouraged L to try with different amounts eg 7p, 5p. (T) modeled how this looks as subtraction. Eg. 10-7=2.

Lee was playing with friends "we have made a rollercoaster." Lee was unhappy that more than 1 child was on at once - (T) encouraged Lee to tell the chn the rule himself what the rule is. Later Lee told (T) he wondered what that meant. "I'm making sure the ride is safe for everyone to use."

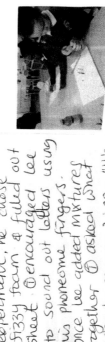

Lee wanted to find England on globe (T) showed him where it is "what's the building?" (T) explained it showed a guard and Big Ben to represent London - the capital city. "oh I remember going there we took 3 buses to get there" he said. Lee thought he lived in North England. (T) explained south of England and showed Lee North, south on the globe.

Lee asked to do a science experiment, he chose fizzy foam & filled out sheet. (T) encouraged Lee to sound out letters using his phoneme fingers. Once Lee added mixtures together (T) asked what was happening? Lee - "Its all fizzing over on the table." (T) asked if he noticed anything else! (T) explained that the lemon juice is an acid & once mixed with the soda, it produces bubbles of carbon dioxide gas. This makes it froth & fizz.

Chn were learning about point balance in P.E (T) encouraged Lee to explore balances on the mat. He challenged himself thinking of a different way he could balance. He held it for 3 seconds.

Lee's friends were playing with a map and beebots. Lee told (T) he wanted a go. (T) encouraged Lee to ask if he & air friends to join. Lee moved the beebot around the map. (T) supported Lee to try 2 and 3 step instruction w/ he had a clear idea of directing them.

(T) noticed Lee's a formation was incorrect. (T) encouraged Lee to practise. He kept starting from the wrong place. (T) modelled and supported Lee to form correctly starting from top. Lee should continue with gross motor skills.

He wanted to move the beebot into a car park. (T) modelled how to reverse the beebot

Fruit smoothies

One of the focus children had had a fruit smoothie at home and was excited by the chance to explain to her friends how to make these at school. The design sheet was completed, with some support from an adult, and a shopping list was written. A group then went to buy the ingredients, adding up the cost of the items as they went round the shop. The children also looked at where in the world the fruit had come from and, with prompts from an adult, they discussed how the items came to be in Enfield! Once back at school, the fruit was prepared and then placed in a blender before everyone had a taste. (Science, design and technology, geography, physical development, numeracy, literacy, PSE.)

Pyramids

These blocks are from Community Playthings. They are designed to support many mathematical concepts and are manufactured with precision.

The pyramid in the photo on the previous page was made with blocks, but the polydrons have also been popular recently and many children have made pyramids with these. When looking on the iPad for images, the Egyptian pyramids became a new fascination. Again, sensitive facilitation by an adult led to the children pondering how such huge structures were built without the machinery that is available today. Books were collected from the library and video clips watched on the iPad. The model seen in the photo was built by a group of four or five children working together and each making a contribution. (Science, design and technology, history, geography, physical development, numeracy, literacy, PSE.)

Wind sock

In this photo, Eren has chosen a project from one of the science books – to make a wind sock. The design sheet can be seen on the table, which he has completed after reading the book and then re-writing and simplifying the instructions so that he fully understands the process. He is now part way through making his model.

Once complete he takes it outside to see how it performs. An adult has explained about wind direction and offered  Eren one of the compasses that are available in the class. Once the trial has been carried out, Eren completes the evaluation on his sheet. Of course, once other children see this event, they too want to have a turn at making something similar and Eren then becomes the 'expert' to whom they refer for advice and help. (Science, design and technology, geography, physical development, numeracy, literacy, PSE.)

Blue Batman mask

Jamie's interest in Batman led to a search on the internet and the discovery of a film clip from the 1960s. In the film, Batman's mask was blue! Jamie was pleased to note that the music was the same though! This led to much discussion and searching in books for other examples of changes to superhero costumes. Jamie decided to re-create a mask for himself and did so independently – remembering to pay for the blue card using money from his money belt. (Design and technology, computing, history, music, physical development, numeracy, literacy, PSE.)

How strong is a Bee–Bot?

A group of boys were playing with the Bee-Bot and decided to see if it could push a block along. 'It's not strong enough!' Baran suggested, 'Let's use **three** Bee-Bots together!'. This took a lot of co-operation and careful timing to get all three Bee-Bots to move at the same time, but eventually they succeeded! (Science, computing, physical development, numeracy, PSE.)

Paper boats

Sasha has learnt how to make paper boats and is happy to share this skill with her friends at school. She gives clear step-by-step instructions, helps if necessary and praises good effort! Several boats are made and then placed in the water tray outdoors to see how long it will take before they sink. (Science, design and technology, physical development, numeracy, literacy, PSE.)

What is inside a dinosaur?

Ismael spent over an hour creating this dinosaur and was determined to make an accurate model. He looked in books and asked for help to read certain words so that he could name the different parts of the body. During the making process, he had to buy the items for his model using the money in his money belt. Once nearly complete, he realised that the dinosaur had no heart or lungs etc. and he then undid the sellotape, made the internal organs, placed them inside the dinosaur and then re-sealed it all. He went on to write a story about his dinosaur (this was a shared process with an adult) and took great pride acting it out to the class and explaining how his model had been made. (Science, design and technology, art and design, history, physical development, numeracy, literacy, PSE.)

I think this picture sums up what we have been trying to achieve in Year One. These two boys have experienced a curriculum and organisation that has given them the freedom to learn in a way that is uniquely suited to them. They have also had superb role models in the adults around them. These adults have ensured that the emotional well-being of the children is protected above all else. These children are confident, independent and empathetic. Thus they do not compete with each other, rather they co-operate and help each other. They understand that they are all different, with different skills and abilities, but that they all want to learn and do the things that interest them. Thus we see here Muhammed helping Robin, just as he has seen adults helping children in this way many times before. He has put aside his own needs in this moment to help his friend. What more can we ask?

This month is often the shortest in the school year, and 2016 was no exception. The children had just three weeks in school in April. As mentioned in the March chapter, the structure of the day has been altered for the final term and this is explained overleaf. The approach to the focus children has also been amended to fit with the new structures. In the environment section, I will look at history and geography. The diary gives some interesting examples to demonstrate how children's interests persist over time and can therefore be a powerful vehicle for learning.

TO DO LIST

- Amend the structure of the day according to staff views and assessments.
- Begin final cycle of focus children (amended – see below).
- Begin final cycle of parent meetings (amended – see below).
- Begin discussions about appropriate structures for Year Two.
- Review the new systems closely by monitoring levels of involvement.

Organisation

A new structure to the day

This was the scene that greeted the children on their return to school after the Easter break. There were no signs or written explanations and therefore discussions were inevitable. Eventually the children determined that it was a crashed spaceship and so the new approach to learning was introduced. This, and many other ideas, came about as a result of three members of staff attending a series of sessions at the Institute of Education around 'The Power of Reading'. The course encourages the use of high-quality picture books as a 'springboard' for activities. We have adapted the approach to offer 'challenges' in all areas of the environment, rather than adult-directed tasks. The first book to be used is *Beegu* and this will last for about four or five weeks. In addition to the challenges, the staff have also now introduced focus literacy and maths tasks (some of which relate to the book).

However, the children still have autonomy and control of their own learning for more than half of the hours in the day. As I write this chapter, it is still unclear exactly what the structure of Year Two will look like in September. In the Easter holiday there has been a door built from the Year Two corridor out into an outdoor area which will be developed for Year Two to use in September. In addition, there will be three new teachers in the year group and this brings challenges, as well as new ideas, new characters and new approaches. At Carterhatch, the approach is always to look at the children and to see how best we can meet their needs. The staff have agreed that they would like to try a slight shift in the provision in Year One; they will monitor this closely and, if successful, this will be a good model to be adopted at the start of Year Two.

Thus the new timetable is as follows:

9–9.35	9.35–10	10–11.45	11.45–12.15	1.25–1.40	1.40–2.50	2.50–3.15
Group reading and handwriting	Literacy input	Free-flow	Phonics	Maths input	Free-flow	Story
(Groups of six or seven reading – supported by an adult)	Based around book and ideas from Power of Reading – challenges introduced	One adult to work with groups – focus on the literacy challenge		One theme to be followed throughout the week (some challenges from book will also be mathematical)	One adult to work with two groups each day to follow up the maths work	

Challenges are optional

As the new structures are introduced, the challenges are optional, but the novelty is enticing and many children opt to do as many as possible. A few examples of the challenges are shown in the diary section starting on page 159. In order to monitor the uptake, the children have been given a laminated number line to keep in their money bag and this is hole-punched each time they complete a challenge (the number lines can be seen on the table in the photo below).

New approach to focus children and parent meetings

In this final term, each child will be a focus child once more. Each week the three children are selected from each class, but no sheet is being sent home this term. During the week, the staff continue to monitor and interact with all the children, as they have done all year. For the focus children, they are paying particular attention to their literacy and numeracy activities, in order to be able to complete a 'report' sheet (see Appendix L) at the end of the week. There is an example of a completed sheet shown below.

   This is shared with the parents after the focus week is complete and this, along with the child's folder, will constitute their end of year report. The only additional items that will be reported to parents are their child's attendance figures.

Name: _Hatun_

Week commencing: _25.4.16_

Carterhatch

Infant School

In English I can:	Photos
• Use expression in my voice when reading a story. • Read my writing aloud to check it makes sense. • Join in a discussion about what I have read. **Next I need to learn:** • using the correct tense verbally and in writing. e.g/ was, were.	
In Maths I can:	
• recognise all coins and notes and their values. • use more than and less than signs to compare values. • Divide by 2 and write the number sentence. **Next I need to learn:** • finding change from pounds.	

In other areas I demonstrate:
Curiosity, imagination, initiative, determination, perseverance, risk-taking, energy, fascination, focus, attention to detail, resilience, enjoyment of challenge, pride, problem solving ability, ability to plan ahead, flexibility, co-operation

This week I have been learning about....	
I was learning about the spac and then I made a earth.	

Setting up the environment

History

If you look carefully at the statements in the current Year One curriculum, they are quite vague and the content is not specified. For example, it talks about 'sorting historical objects from "then" and "now"', but it does not specify which objects. Similarly, it mentions 'identifying some similarities and differences between different ways of life in different periods' but does not specify which aspects or from which periods. Therefore, the environment is not the key factor here. Rather the staff and the availability of

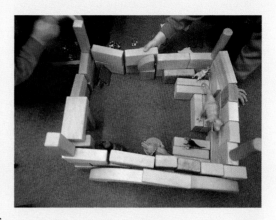

research materials are important to tap into any interest that arises, in order to exploit the 'historical' aspect to the event. For example, the photo above shows a model which the children called a 'dinosaur museum'. This led to discussions about dinosaurs and why they are in museums, why they can't be seen anywhere in the world and what the world might have been like when there were dinosaurs here. Immediately, much of the history curriculum had been covered and for those children that were playing with this model, the historical concepts were clarified. There are such events occurring daily and a few have been mentioned in earlier chapters – ordering photos and items from home, the batman mask, dinosaur questions, repairing an old teddy.

In addition, the staff have set up an area in one of the classes, in which they have placed some objects to entice the children to investigate and ask questions. Cameras, phones and toys from various eras are quite easy to source and these are things that are familiar to children aged five and six.

Whatever the curriculum we are given, we must look at the children in our own settings and decide what is appropriate and meaningful to them. In the photo on the

next page, the children had noticed how dirty the windows were and wanted to clean them. Since there were no cleaning products available, an adult suggested they use newspaper and vinegar like they used to do in the 'olden days'. A discussion then began and the iPads were used to investigate before the children decided to try the method for themselves. They were quite impressed with the results.

Geography

The environment and resources are more critical for the coverage of the geography curriculum and so these have been adapted and added to, both indoors and outside. Again, however, the adults are the key to the geographical aspects of play being exploited. Thus we have seen how the football fanatics were encouraged to find out

Alice, the adult in this photo, has placed herself with her back to a wall. This means that she is able to interact with these two boys, but can also scan the whole room.

where their favourite teams came from and the surfers were encouraged to research the best surfing beaches. In order to facilitate such research, the iPads are often used but there are also globes, atlases and books indoors, as well as large purpose-made outdoor maps on the wall in the garden (see photo on page 77).

Another aspect of the geography curriculum covers knowledge about the local area, the school and how to improve it. The children go out into the local area often and, in many cases, this is to buy things to improve the school. Thus they have learnt where the pet shop is and have added guinea pigs to enhance the environment; they have built a pond; they have been to the garden centre and are trying to develop the vegetable patch. When cooking, they often go to buy the ingredients and then discuss where they have come from and how they got to England. The trips to their swimming lessons take them slightly further afield as well as allowing them to experience travelling on a bus. With the focus children, it is up to staff to 'tap into' all the aspects of learning that the child's interests offer. By focusing on just a few children each week, this can be done in depth and in a meaningful way. As stated before, a meaningful, personal piece of learning is worth so much more, and has so much more impact, than whole-class teaching. In this final term, the books are being chosen carefully to ensure they have the widest possible appeal and also have the potential to cover a wide range of subjects. As always, we are monitoring the levels of involvement and continue to give the children a great deal of freedom during each day. In this way, the adults are still able to 'tap into' current interests that might arise outside of the 'planned' events.

Diary extracts: examples of development and learning

WHAT TO LOOK OUT FOR

- Children continue to display high levels of involvement during free-flow sessions.
- Children now display high levels of involvement during adult-led tasks.
- Some children opt for, and are engaged by, challenges.
- Children are more aware of their learning and what they need to do to improve.
- Long-term interests continue to fascinate individual children.

The diary sections in these last few chapters will be divided into two sections – some describing child-initiated events from free-flow play sessions and others describing some of the events that occurred as a result of the challenges that were placed in the environment. The adult-led focus tasks for literacy and maths will not be described. There are enough books, blogs and Facebook pages describing such tasks and I do not feel the need to add to that mountain. However, I would remind practitioners to monitor the levels of involvement whatever the activity – if they are very low, then stop the activity as it is clearly a waste of time and effort.

Another dead mouse!

If you have read *The Nursery Year in Action*, you will know that this same cohort of children found a dead mouse in the nursery garden, so I was intrigued to see how they would react to this event two years' later. The discussions revolved around signs of death and they quickly concluded that it was not asleep because it was not breathing. Next was the challenge of moving it off the stage without touching it. Zack immediately ran off to fetch a box and trowel and manoeuvred the mouse into the box.

Next the children quickly agreed that the mouse should be buried. A hole had already been dug in the investigation area and so the mouse was placed in there and then covered with soil. Several children then wanted to decorate the area and they used daisies, dandelions and buttercups to do this.

Finally the children started to talk about the family of the mouse and how they must be worried about him. They decided to leave a 'note' in the hole. Kayra dicated the message and Alfie wrote it carefully. They realised that they needed to write it on a piece of wood as paper would not last outdoors. They wrote 'To Micky's mum and dad. Micky is dead. He is buried here. From children.'.

I was in another school recently when a dead mouse was found in their garden. The site manager was called and the mouse removed immediately. Huge learning opportunity missed.

A wormery

As mentioned, many of the worms are being fed to the chickens but Rayan decided to keep some and, after investigating on the iPad, decided to make a wormery. At this point an adult was able to provide the correct container and then Rayan continued to work independently. He even wrote instructions for other children to follow if they wanted to build one.

Interests persist – sewing

The photo on the left below shows Alara in nursery with a bag that she made with adult support.

In Year One, she still loves to make things and sewing remains an activity that challenges and interests her. She can now do this independently and with great skill.

Chicks in Reception

The children in Year One have heard that there are eggs in Reception and that these are going to hatch. Several children asked to go and see them and then visited each day for a week, noting changes and cracks in the eggs until finally the chicks were hatched. They continued to visit and make notes about the changes that they observed. Melisa even got to hold one of the new-borns!

Money, money, money!

The money belts are still in use every day. The children now have 40p per day and the introduction of this activity has seen dramatic progress in the chidren's abilities in recognising, combining and calculating with money. It is also now absolutely the norm. The children come in each day and put on their money belt. They have no anxiety about this 'game' and often play with money, using amounts way beyond their 40p as seen in these pictures. They are also very familiar with Numicon and sometimes use this resource to support their calculations.

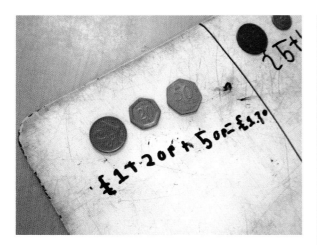

A mathematical 'Wow!' moment

The 'Wow!' moments are still being recorded – sometimes just with a note and sometimes with a photo. The photo overleaf is one such moment. Actually, it was nearer to an hour than a moment. An hour in which Adelle grasped the concept of multiplication, was thrilled by this discovery and motivated to do harder and harder examples. No one had told her to do this. Rachel joined her and observed for a while but Adelle was working independently.

This sort of learning is so much more powerful than that which is forced onto children when they are not interested.

On the whiteboard it says:

7 X 7 = 49
7 X 5 = 35
9 X 6 = 54
6 X 5

Animals

With rabbits, guinea pigs, chicks, chickens, worms, mice, mini-beasts and pond-life, the children in Year One are constantly aware of the animals and their needs. They continue to be responsible for the feeding and cleaning of these creatures – something else that has become the norm for them.

Ruth and Maisie

A very special visitor came into school this month too. Ruth returned with her baby Maisie to visit the children. The children saw Ruth just before she went on maternity leave and they have now seen her with her baby. Science is not all in books!

Beegu

As stated, there are challenges around the environment that the children can choose to do if they wish. Many of them have done so and with some surprising results. The book, Beegu, is about an alien who crashes on earth and the challenges relate to this. Some are indoors, such as the one shown below. The challenges are presented in stands around the class.

The challenges are displayed in stands, both indoors and outside, such as the one shown here on the table.

In addition, many of the challenges are outside, for example: 'Can you show Beegu how to keep fit?'.

Megan responded to another challenge, saying that she thought Beegu would like to taste ice cream and that she would make some for him. When trying to decide on a flavour, an adult suggested she make a tally chart and ask several children their opinion about this. Chocolate was the most popular, Megan completed her design and method sheet and the ice cream was then made.

Clipboards are available outdoors so that children who are more comfortable outside can do any written work without the paper blowing away.

The link to space and the planets within the Beegu book means that many children can continue to explore this area of interest. The children have done lots of research in non-fiction books and have made (to mention just a few) satellites, model planets, representations of the solar system and spaceships. Some children are fascinated by space and planets and this has led them to take these challenges and become deeply involved with them.

The 'tally' underneath the coloured squares shows that this idea has been introduced to the children. How they choose to use this skill will vary from child to child according to their interests.

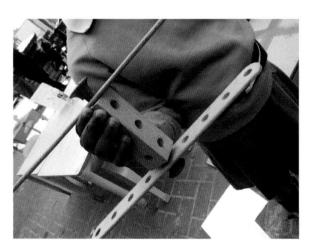

In the photo above, the challenge can be seen on the table. These children have chosen to use modrock to complete the task.

While some children are fascinated by space, others are still drawn to the creative and imaginative aspects of learning. The book, Beegu, along with the challenges selected, mean that these children too can become deeply involved in something that interests them. Thus Melisa was able to spend nearly a whole week creating her own model of Beegu, along with a story box in which to act out related stories, some of which she recorded and acted out with some friends. Adelle chose drawing and a caption – again a challenge that she relished and enjoyed doing.

'Beegu's world has delicate stars that twinkle.'

In another challenge the children were asked to think about what Beegu would see on earth. Zinar and Abdulkadir put their own interpretation onto this challenge, creating a pair of glasses which, when you put them on, showed what Beegu would see!

The children can do the challenges alone or with friends. This removes the competitive element and encourages co-operation. It also allows different children to excel as the challenges draw on a variety of skills and interests.

In the final example we can see how one challenge led to learning in numerous areas of the curriculum. Efsun took the challenge of choosing where Beegu had landed and decided on Egypt. The country was then found on the giant world map and investigated in non-fiction books. This led to a link to pyramids – an existing interest for Efsun and further learning about this subject for her. It also led her to use polydrons, a construction toy that she had not used before and which she found difficult to manipulate. However, the interest in the subject was the motivation that supported her perseverance and eventual success. This, in turn, led to her making a net with card to create a pyramid that she could keep.

These examples show learning in all subject areas. As mentioned earlier, I have not included the literacy or numeracy focus tasks, but I should reassure the reader that literacy and numeracy are occurring everywhere too. I have chosen, in this chapter, to focus on activities that relate to other subjects. However, even within the examples given, you can see how the children are reading constantly, they are using money to buy resources, many of the activities have mathematical elements within them and most involve some writing – be that a plan, a list, a report, a recipe or an evaluation. These children are getting a truly 'rounded' education – something which I think is becoming more and more unusual in England at this time. The new structure to the days and week seems to be working very well. The children are still fully committed to their learning, involved and excited. When I

talk to the teachers who have taught Year One in a more formal way in previous years, they report that the children this year are making similar or better progress, with attainment that is equal to, and for many better than, previous years. However, the most noticeable difference is the behaviour, particularly of the boys. Their self-esteem has been protected and they have not been pressurised or stressed. They have not been 'turned off' learning, they love their learning and therefore the behaviour issues are virtually non-existent. Happy boys in Year One – that has to be the best 'Wow!' moment ever!

9 | May

May, like April, is a short month in school – with the half term break and several bank holidays as well. The new timetable, introduced in April, is continuing as the staff feel it has been successful and so there is little new organisational information to give. However, at this time in the academic year, there is a tendency in all year groups to start to panic about results. This 'panic' and fear often leads to formalised, inappropriate practices being introduced as a 'quick fix'. Practitioners feel very isolated and believe that in every other school, things are different – they are not! We need to stick with what we know is right and the results will come. Therefore, in this chapter, I will give space to look at how speech and language are developed throughout the year group, as a reminder that these children are at the earliest stages of their education. Similarly the practical application of maths is a life skill – writing out pages of sums is not! This book gives many examples of how children use maths in their play and practitioners must continue to observe, note and value this. In the environment section, I will give a detailed account of how the growing area has been developed with a simple guide for practitioners wishing to try this venture in their own setting. The diary section will again cover the two aspects of the children's play: their child-initiated play and the play they pursue when completing challenges. The work around the book *Beegu* was completed and a new book introduced – *The Lonely Beast*. The diary gives some examples of some of the challenges from both books.

TO DO LIST

- Continue final cycle of focus children.
- Continue final cycle of parent meetings, including report discussions.
- Discuss and amend provision if necessary.
- Continue to focus on speech and language.
- Continue to focus on practical application of maths skills.

Organisation

Speech and language

Communication is key to all learning and we must keep this as a priority, whatever age children we are working with. Humans can survive without phonics, but communication is a life skill. In spite of the pressure to develop phonics, we must not neglect speech and language development. In June 2015, the Department for Education produced a report on the evaluation of the impact of the phonics screening test for Year One children in England. Their own report concludes that **'the evidence suggests that the introduction of the check has had an impact on pupils' attainment in phonics, but not (or not yet) on their attainment in literacy.'** Whatever we focus on in schools will improve – be that phonics or dance or science or social skills. Education systems, generally, tend to focus on what is easy to measure. However, it is up to schools to decide what is most important for young children, rather than what is easiest to measure or what is the current fad of the government. It is easy to show a correlation between two

Recently I was speaking to a student teacher who had spent two weeks in a school with a very formal approach. She was disturbed by the fact that no children were laughing. It did not 'feel right'. My advice to her was to trust her instincts. It is not right! There is something seriously disturbing about a school without laughter.

events – for example a school might conclude 'We changed the flooring in the corridors and the behaviour improved.'. This is a correlation – it is not a causal link – there are a thousand other things that could have impacted on behaviour in that period. In the case of phonics, the government are struggling even to find a correlation between phonics and literacy. A focus on speech and language would be far more likely to bring the results that they aspire to. However, it would not bring profits to the companies producing the synthetic phonic programmes and perhaps this is why it is being overlooked. We, as a profession, however, need to reclaim our education system from the government and focus on what we know to be truly valuable. It is only by doing so that we will see the long-term results that we value – young people with a love of learning and the skills necessary to be independent learners. Social skills must be top of the list (discussed throughout this book) with speech and language a close second.

If two children have a conversation, it is evidence of their personal and social skills, as well as their communication skills. The two areas are very closely linked – indeed all areas of development are dependent on good personal and social skills, i.e. the 'can-do' attitude that allows children to take risks and learn. This emphasis on the well-being of the children is evident throughout the book. Once this is established, the children are in a state of mind where new learning is possible and pursued. But how can speech and language can be encouraged and supported?

1. The first point to make is that we assume that all **children want to communicate** – it is a human instinct. With this in mind, practitioners can work to do everything possible to facilitate and support this instinct.
2. Accepting that children want to talk, the priority, when they are in school, is to **ensure their well-being**. Stress is a huge barrier to learning – sending children into 'fight or flight' mode. Children need to be relaxed and confident as it is in this state that they are open to the experiences on offer.
3. Even with good well-being, children still need **something to talk about!** A major part of the practitioner's role is to provide an environment and experiences that will entice the children to talk. The provision should be designed to get every child deeply engaged in something and therefore the environment needs to offer a **wide variety of open-ended resources**, accessible to all children which can be used in numerous different ways. Blocks are a great example – a child who is fascinated by motorbikes can make and **talk** about a motorbike, and other children can make and **talk** about a castle!

   Outdoor provision is particularly important for supporting talk. Not only are there exciting things outside, but there is also space and the possibility of not being heard, which for some children is very important. They want to talk, but might not want adults listening. Outside they can build a den or hide in the bushes to have a 'private' chat with their friends. Also there are often more 'risky' (and therefore appealing) experiences outside, such as woodwork, rope swings, climbing equipment – and these often evoke lots of excited talk – discussing the challenges and problems that these experiences bring. We have also seen how animals, which are usually outside, offer a first-hand experience that many children would not have at home – these then also provoke talk.

   Photos of children inspire them to talk. Children love looking at pictures of themselves and their family and telling friends and staff about them. There are so many other simple, hands-on activities that inspire talk, including **trips into the local area, cooking, the weather, plants and mini-beasts**.
4. As mentioned above, certain areas outdoors (and other quiet, cosy areas indoors) give opportunities for the children to talk to each other without adults. However, the **timetable and staff organisation must ensure that adults are free to interact with**

children as much as possible. The time when the children are **playing** is the time when they are **learning** and is the time when the adults are **teaching.** The adults' main role is to interact with the children and move their learning on. They should be looking for 'teachable moments' and then interacting with the children. A large proportion of these interactions involve teaching children to communicate and talk. Adults need to be constantly alert to ensure that as many opportunities as possible are spotted and exploited to develop the children's language – thus maximising their progress.

5. In order to ensure the best quality of interactions (teaching) there are a few **principles** that practitioners can follow:

   a) **Adults should go to the children.** When a child has found something that interests them, they become deeply involved. It is critical that the adults go to where the children are involved and interested because it is in this state that they are far more likely to have something they **want to talk about.**

   b) Once with the children, the **adults should watch and wait** for the moment when they can interact in a way that will support the learning, rather than spoil the moment. Waiting is very difficult for practitioners, but it is the key when trying to promote language development. Let the **children initiate the conversation** and it is far more likely to flow.

   c) Children are experts at 'reading' adults and they need to know that **the adults like the children and are genuinely interested in them** as unique, fascinating individuals. Without this trust, any learning (including language development) will falter.

Once the staff spot a teachable moment when they can enhance language development they can employ **numerous specific strategies to support speech** as follows:

Reflect back	Reflect back what the child has said (having waited for the child to speak first!) to ensure they have understood correctly. So for example Zara says 'baby eat' and the adult responds 'The baby is eating?'
Scaffold and model	In the example above, the response from the adult also then includes **scaffolding and modelling** – adding extra words to the phrase and modelling correct sentence structure.
Use gestures and signing, such as Makaton	In this case, if the child is at an early stage of development in spoken English, the adult should accompany the verbal response with the use of **Makaton**. This is a signing system that can be introduced to **all** children. It particularly supports communication for children with English as an additional language, children who are shy and children with language delay, but it also allows every child to communicate with every other child in a setting.
Tailor the response to the unique child	The adult responses need to be **tailored to the unique child**. Adults need to know the children very well in order to ensure that their response is appropriate – giving the child the correct amount of new learning – not too much and not too little. In this case the adult knew that Zara was sometimes using the article 'the' and so reminded her of this and also introduced the suffix 'ing' as new learning. For another child, the adult response should be different because they would assess and respond according to their knowledge of *that child*.

Avoid too many questions. Use 'I wonder . . .'	Staff should **avoid too many questions** (questions can be stressful for children), but rather they should **ponder**. For example, Jaden says 'Look! My hat is gone!' and the adult responds 'Oh your hat is over the fence. **I wonder** how we can get it back.' The response has involved reflecting back, scaffolding, modelling and pondering – all tailored to this particular child. In this way the adult **invites but does not insist on further communication**.
Commentate	For a child who is more reticent to speak, adults should **commentate** as the child plays – again tailored to the particular child. For example they might say 'Oh you have a cuboid . . . You have added some fabric – and some legs. I wonder if you are making a bed.' The child will be hearing the language and might use it later when the adult is not there.
Direct teaching	Sometimes an interaction will involve some **direct teaching**. For example, Amir says 'I want this.' (*He points to the drill that another child is using*). The adult responds 'This is called a "drill". Can you say that . . . "drill"?'. Amir repeats 'drill'.

All these strategies should be used to **support the children in communicating with each other as well as with the adults**.

In brief: ensure well-being and ensure engagement – then watch, wait and interact according to the needs of each unique child.

Setting up the environment

The growing area

The photo opposite was taken in September when the children were helping to prepare the growing area in Year One. The following grid gives a month-by-month explanation of how to develop a growing area. The benefits have been explained in various sections of the book, not least with regard to the scientific aspects of learning that it delivers. It also encourages the children to consider their local environment and to take responsibility for this. If you plan to do this in any year group, I would advise having the growing area in your usual outdoor area – i.e. in your garden, rather than in another part of the school grounds. If it is in your garden, you will see it every day and then any jobs that need doing will be evident immediately. It also means that children can work in the area independently, without having to be escorted by any adult. I would suggest that you need a 'champion' for this to be successful – an adult (staff or volunteer) who will take ownership of the project and ensure it is kept on track.

Month, tasks and comments	Photos and comments
September Select an area to develop. (If the area is concrete, then you will need deeper soil.) Order soil and seeds. Find or request logs (from your local Parks Department). Use two layers of sleepers if you have a concrete base. Dig up grass or bushes. Place logs or sleepers as boundary. Fill area with soil or prepare existing soil.	 Wellington boots are nearby along with baskets in which to place shoes. In Year One, there was a raised bed already in existence but it was full of rocks and rubbish. The children and staff spent many days digging and sieving the soil and adding fresh soil.
October Add access paths (scaffold planks, decking or stepping stones are fine). Add trellis and/or sticks to support tall plants. Fix tools nearby (on the fence in this photo). Add a compost bin to the area. This year the children added 'scarecrows' to try and keep the chickens out of the area. (See models attached to fence.)	

November and December

Plant fruit trees (if you plan to have these).

Plant garlic.

Herbs can be planted at any time during the year.

January

Plant fruit bushes – strawberries, raspberries, etc.

Plant broad beans in pots outside.

If the children can be involved in buying the seeds, then even better. We are lucky to have a shop near to school.

February

If mild, plant carrots, parsnips, onions, lettuces and radishes.

Put the beans from the pots into the soil.

March

Plant cabbages and leeks.

April

Put straw around strawberry plants.

Sow seeds in pots such as marrows, courgettes, tomatoes and cucumbers.

Plant potatoes – these are best grown in big bags.

May

Move the plants from the pots to outside or buy (or be given) established plants.

A few items might be ready to pick – e.g. herbs, lettuce, etc.

Support tall bushes with canes and ties.

Plant sweetcorn.

June

Water, water, water!

Water from a water butt is the best for the plants.

July

Harvest as much as possible before the children leave for the summer break.

Some produce will be ready when the new children arrive in September.

Allow the children to taste as much of the produce as possible. Vegetable soup is easy and lots of children will be interested in getting involved.

Potatoes and beans should be ready to be harvested.

Strawberries!

Diary extracts: examples of development and learning

WHAT TO LOOK OUT FOR

- Children are pursuing 'lines of enquiry' which can last a few days or longer.
- Children are enjoying some structured lessons.
- Children continue to be fully engaged during free-flow sessions.
- Children start to anticipate the move to Year Two.

As mentioned, the diary section has two aspects – the first is looking at events that the children initiate in their free-flow time – events unrelated to their challenges or to the adult-led sessions that are now taking place. The second part of the diary looks at a few of the challenges around the books that are being used this month, and how the children interpreted these.

Gymnastics

Although the children do now have structured PE lessons, their physical development is progressing throughout the sessions of free-flow play as well. In the photo opposite, the girls have used a tarpaulin to cover the bark – thus creating a smooth surface over the soft surface – safe and comfortable! They are also teaching each other – without any learning objectives or lesson plans.

Responsibilities are enjoyed

The children now relish the chance to get into the animal pens. The fear that was evident at the start of the year in some children has (in almost every case) disappeared. The children are proud of their ability to pick up the chickens, deal with the 'poo' and provide a clean environment for the animals. When they are older, this is the sort of experience that will stay with them, that will have a long-lasting impact and will teach them that some activities might be daunting to begin with, but that they can bring surprising satisfaction. The chicks that were hatched in the Reception classes have now joined the bigger chickens in their coop. Extra responsibility and extra interest for the children.

These children are still so young

The atmosphere in Year One at the start of the year was one of energy, purposefulness, happiness, excitement, curiosity and interest. This has not changed. Each time I walk through the Year One environment, it strikes me again – just how happy these children are. A visitor this month commented; 'I teach Year One and my children are quite happy to come to school and they get on with what we ask them to do. But this is inspirational and a real eye-opener for me. The children here love what they are doing. It is incredible!'. There is a definite difference in the organisation now and at any time, there is an adult in each room, working with a group, leading a literacy or maths activity. However, all around them – indoors and outside – there are children playing and learning independently. The photo below shows such a group. There is a table nearby where an adult is working with another

group, but these young children still have long periods in which they can select what to do. These children have chosen the polydrons and the brio construction set to play with. Both these pieces of equipment demand focus, persistence and a level of dexterity that is beyond most children in the early years. It engages these Year One children and challenges them. If we could scan their brains at this moment, we would see new synapses forming. If we talked to them we would learn about their designs, their games, their ideas. These young children are still loving their experience of school. For me, that is the best measure of success.

Beegu challenges continue

The photo below shows a completed puppet. The children still have the option to complete the challenges or not, but most are relishing the tasks and enjoy bringing the completed 'evidence' to show an adult and have their number line hole-punched.

Mariyah is holding up her puppet as evidence that she has completed this challenge. In her right hand, you can see her laminated number line, which will now be hole-punched as a record of this.

This challenge had a second part which was to create and film a puppet show and Mariyah and Efsun can be seen on the next page co-operating in this task. They are also using the iPad, thus including ICT in their play. The levels of involvement are as high as ever, even though the children have to complete the challenges independently. This requires careful planning by the adults – if the challenges are too hard, the children will not be able to complete them independently and if they are too easy, we would not see these high levels of involvement. At this point in the year, this approach has been very successful, and this is because the children have had three years to develop the characteristics of effective learning that they need. They also have the literacy and numeracy skills required to read and carry out the challenges. They also have their friends to help them. The sense of competition about how many challenges they can complete does not mean that they are becoming selfish. Rather, they complete the challenges with, or alongside, their friends so that they can all get the next hole punched in their number line!

There is little evidence, as yet, to show what the long-term effects of 'screens' will be on our children. Studies are ongoing, but we do not have to wait for the results. Our instincts tell us that screen games and 'apps' are addictive and they also remove people from 'social' interaction. Many people in the highest positions in 'tech' companies do not let their own children have iPads. In school, we are careful in how screen technology is used – ensuring that it is used in ways that might not be the norm at home.

The 'Power of Reading' course gives much emphasis to how the books are introduced and read to the children. This results in every child being interested because the numerous aspects within the content of the books are highlighted and explored. Several copies are available in each class, along with several copies of supporting non-fiction texts. So, for example, with Beegu, there are many books about the planets and space to entice some children to engage. Others are intrigued by the story and others by the plight of the character within the book. The measure of success is scenes such as the two below – where individuals and groups are found reading in various areas of the class and garden.

The Beast needs a friend!

The second book that was introduced was 'The Lonely Beast' and one of the challenges involved making a friend for 'The Beast'. Many children opted to use plasticine and the results were colourful and varied. The children were able to put their own individuality into the design.

I think these three photos are a lovely way to end this chapter – they reflect the Year One children at Carterhatch this year and they convey the atmosphere in the year group – the energy, excitement, happiness, individuality, skill and purpose. The staff are exhausted and have a short break before the last two months in school. At this time of year, teachers feel like split personalities – trying to focus on their current cohort as well as preparing for the new academic year. Never a dull moment!

At the time of writing this book, June in England is plagued by the spectre of the phonics screening test which takes place this month. However, the children in the photo above, like all the other children in Year One at Carterhatch, are unaware of the test and do not feel anxious about it. In the previous chapter I explained that even the Department of Education has not seen any improvement in literacy skills since the introduction of the test. My hope is that it will be boycotted in years to come and, eventually, abandoned. Other events in June included a trip to the zoo as a 'springboard' for the introduction of a third book – *One day on our blue planet . . . in the Savannah* – and a special delivery to the outdoor area!

TO DO LIST

- Complete the final cycle of focus children.
- Complete the final cycle of parent meetings.
- Begin plans for transition – both for Reception children coming up and current children moving to Year Two.

- Start completing end of year assessments.
- Review and order any resources that need replacing or re-stocking for the new academic year.

Organisation

Timetable remains unchanged

The timetable that was introduced in April remains the same. I am including it again in this chapter as a reminder to the reader that, although I am not describing the adult-led sessions in depth, they are happening. I stress again that I do not feel the need to explain what is happening in such sessions as they are the more 'traditional' type lessons and there are numerous books available to support staff in the delivery of these. However, I do not want to give the impression that we are neglecting to give the children the basic skills that they need in order to learn. The main message, however, is that literacy and maths are tools that a child should learn to use in order to pursue learning in an area that interests them. At the same time, in these latter months of Year One, we are introducing some focused literacy and numeracy tasks, partly to ensure that all the children practise certain skills and also in order to prepare them for the slightly more structured day that will be delivered in Year Two.

9–9.35	9.35–10	10–11.45	11.45–12.15	1.25–1.40	1.40–2.50	2.50–3.15
Group reading and handwriting	Literacy input	Free-flow	Phonics	Maths input	Free-flow	Story
(Groups of six or seven reading – supported by an adult)	Based around book and ideas from Power of Reading – challenges introduced	One adult to work with groups – focus on the literacy challenge		One theme to be followed throughout the week (some challenges from book will also be mathematical)	One adult to work with two groups each day to follow up the maths work	

Phonics screening test

The timetables for each term have included dedicated time for staff to deliver a systematic programme of phonics, following letters and sounds. This is combined with cued articulation and most of the children (those who came through our nursery) have now had three years of this programme. As this book goes to print, I can report that 75 per cent of the cohort passed the test this year, which was the highest ever for the school. However, for me, a measure of the **personal, social and emotional development** of the cohort would be far more important and would show a 100 per cent pass rate!

Setting up the environment

Mud kitchen

I am often asked if the Year One environment is very different to that of nursery or Reception and there is some discussion of this in the September chapter. The answer is not simple and the 'mud kitchen' is a good example of the complexities of child development and play. In this picture, we see Kaan playing on his own in this area. In nursery and Reception, he rarely went into the muddy area, but in Year One, on this day, he found it deeply engaging. When I visit other settings, practitioners often say to me 'Is it ok to have . . . in this year group?' My answer is always the same: 'Does it feel right?'. Practitioners have been so 'knocked' in recent years that they find it very difficult to trust their own judgement any longer. They want the simple answers, the answers that will satisfy the head teacher,

the early years advisers, the governors, Ofsted and the parents. However, my advice is very simple: 'Get it right for the children and you won't go far wrong.' The look on Kaan's face tells us that this is right for Kaan at this moment. That is all we need to know.

In this area, there is mud (in an old disused sandpit); containers – saucepans, bowls, bottles, watering cans, plates, cups; utensils – gardening tools as well as kitchen utensils; seating; tables; shelving; and a water butt. This is not a definitive list – add whatever you can find and see what engages the children. The chance to mix mud with water, bark, grass, leaves, etc. leads to infinite possibilities. Trust the children and follow their lead. If you don't have a ready supply of mud, you might have to buy it, but it is not expensive and a cubic metre can be delivered from local garden centres.

Transition from Reception to Year One

If at all possible, June is the perfect time to begin transition work with the Reception children. Young children can easily develop anxieties about future events, such as moving to Year One, and a short visit to their new environment can allay their fears and actually make them excited about the move. Such visits do not have to be long (half an hour is fine) and they do not have to be planned. The children in our Reception classes are used to organising their own play and, therefore, short visits to Year One during which they can explore, observe and play are ideal.

Diary extracts: examples of development and learning

WHAT TO LOOK OUT FOR

- Parents are delighted by the progress that their children have made.
- Many of the youngest children make sudden leaps in their development.
- Children continue to speculate about Year Two.
- Reception children begin to visit Year One.

The Lonely Beast

One of the challenges from the new book was to 'make a model of the beast'. Because there are numerous materials available, the children used a variety of methods to complete the challenge, as the photos on the next page show; a mask, a clay model, using mod-rock and sewing fabric.

PSE focus in many challenges

The storyline in the book is about a beast who is not in his home area and therefore has no family or friends around him. The book lends itself to a focus on PSE – as seen in the May chapter when the children made a 'friend' for the Beast. Many of the adult input sessions involve discussions about feelings, difficult journeys, not understanding a language and not being welcomed. Some of the challenges that were available during the free-flow sessions included ideas on how to make the Beast feel happier. Ideas included singing or dancing for him and making a party. These led on to the creation of new songs and dances, designing and making party food and organising party games. The top photo, opposite, shows a group of girls outside writing a list of party games that the Beast might enjoy. The challenge is being completed as a group and the girls are all contributing to the task.

The sense of co-operation and collaboration is evident in every area and it is so refreshing to see children who feel education is not a competition, rather a wonderful journey. In the second photo there are children who have chosen to work independently. One is working on drawings of various emotions and both have completed a design sheet for some party food. This is not just a 'paper exercise'. They will get to make the food and eat it!

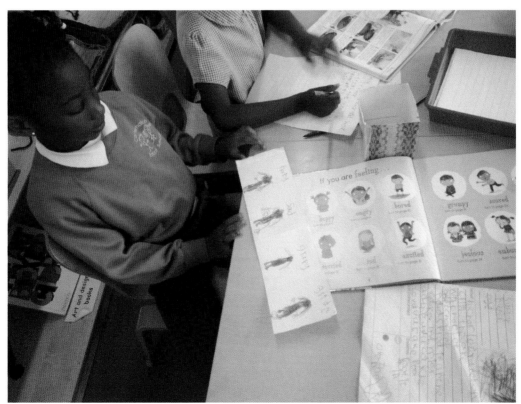

Obstacles

Another challenge involved thinking about the obstacles that the Beast might have come across on his journey. Many are described in the book, but the challenge was to create others within the outdoor environment of Year One. Again, the open-ended nature of the challenge invited collaboration and discussion.

Adult-led but still engaging

As explained, the children are having some adult-led sessions, in line with the work suggested by the Power of Reading course. However, the levels of involvement are maintained by the way the sessions are delivered. Even when there is a whole-class input (during the literacy session as indicated on the timetable – see page 187), this is often a very short input and then a group task – as the picture below shows, this is not always at tables and is not about children working on their own. Indeed the conversations and collaboration are as important as the literacy elements.

This carpet area is large enough for the whole class to sit down comfortably. However, when this is not necessary, the area is well used as the shelving units have been placed around it. These act as a border (protecting the area and any models or activities being made or carried out there) and also provide accessible, appropriate storage for the resources.

A new arrival in the garden

When my colleague, Ruth, mentioned that she was having to get rid of her piano, and that it was going to be destroyed, I immediately suggested that it could be delivered to school, instead of the dump. As explained, we use extra thick tarpaulins (from Costco) and I knew that we could keep the piano dry. I was aware that it might get damp and that it might

only last a few years in school, but since it was heading to the dump anyway, I definitely thought it was worth the effort. Once delivered, the staff explained that only two children at a time could use the piano, and that they were to play gently with their fingers (holding their hand in a 'crab-like' position). Some children quickly began to pick out tunes and the notes for 'Happy Birthday' were written out for the children to follow. Other simple nursery rhyme tunes were soon added.

I am always on the lookout for free 'gifts'. Over the years, I have been given hundreds of small items, but I have also been given a caravan, a boat, horse saddles and now – a piano!

A trip to the zoo

The final book that the staff will be introducing is *One day on our blue planet . . . in the Savannah.*

The photo above reflects how zoos are changing – reinforced glass allows the children a clear view of the lions and the environment for the lions is clearly preferable to a tiny cage. The experience of a day out includes travelling by coach, eating outdoors, following instructions, taking care of belongings – as well as seeing many animals. Such trips are complex to organise and Jacqui was meticulous in her planning. But the experience will be remembered for years to come and the learning is almost impossible to measure. The work that the children produced in the weeks following their outing was impressive and the children were fully engaged with the subject matter, in a way that they would not have been without this initial experience. Some of this work is described in the next chapter.

With the final month of the academic year approaching, the staff team are starting to realise just how successful the year has been. The 'data' this year is not going to help us prove just how successful it has been. This is because there is very little data available. Life beyond levels is still a whole new arena for schools in England at this time. We have the phonics screening test result and we also have some tracking data for literacy and maths (discussed briefly in the next chapter) but it is not comparable with previous years. However, the emotional well-being of the children and their levels of involvement are superb and that is my measure of success in any setting, whatever the age of the child.

11 July

In this final chapter, I will explain the transition work that was continued from June to make smooth transitions from, and into, Year One. I will also look at the progress that the children have made, with the information that is available. In the environment section, I will explain what our review of the year has taught us and any changes that we are proposing for September in light of discussions. The diary section gives a few examples of events that occurred as a result of the challenges from the new book about the Savannah.

TO DO LIST

- Review the year, including the environment, the timetable, the organisation.
- Induct any new staff, so they are ready for the start of the year in September.
- Complete transition work for Reception children coming into Year One.
- Complete transition work for current children moving into Year Two.
- Ensure all parent meetings have been completed.
- Prepare and hand in any end of year assessments that the school requires.
- Order any new stock or resources in light of discussions.

Organisation

Transition

In an ideal world, transition would be an ongoing process. If successful, it would mean that the children would be totally familiar with their new class environment, staff and way of working. There are many ways that this can be organised, by ensuring events in which children move from year group to year group are the norm throughout the year. This is an area that we are striving to develop at Carterhatch and we have gone a long way towards achieving this for the nursery children moving into Reception. However, for the older children there is still a lot of work to be done. It has been made even more difficult this year due to high staff movement. In Year Two, for example, there will be three new teachers and only one of them has been available to be in school for any great length of time this term. Also, although the Year Two environment has had some initial work done on it (with doors being put in to access an outdoor area), the change of staffing means that any further work has had to be delayed until the holiday. However, the children in Year One have had a year in which they have grown in independence, confidence and resilience. Therefore, whatever Year Two offers, they will be as well prepared as we could possibly hope for. Similarly, in Year One in September, there will be three different teachers. Ruth is still on maternity leave, Rachel is moving to a new job and Jacqui is going on maternity leave at the end of this term. However, the Reception children have had several visits into Year One and any fears have been allayed. In fact, they are very excited about the prospect of spending more time in the new environment. Their visits have re-assured them that they will continue to have the autonomy that they have been used to and the environment will offer them further challenges and interest, along with familiar areas as well.

Progress

There is little comparable quantitative (numerical) data available at present, since the National Curriculum levels have been removed. Ofsted are expecting schools to develop their own methods for tracking progress and they do not define how this should be done. For this cohort, we do still have the foundation stage profile data and so this can be used as a starting point. Most of the children in Year One were in our Reception year but about ten per cent of the year group are new to the school.

Looking at all 90 children in Year One now, at the end of Reception, **60 per cent of them achieved a good level of development**, as defined by the assessment requirements in England at this time. This means that 60 per cent of the children achieved the 12 early learning goals covering personal, social and emotional development, communication and language development, physical development, literacy development and mathematical development.

At the end of Year One:

> 75 per cent of the cohort passed the phonics screening test (which is the only piece of numerical data that is submitted to the DfE).

The teacher assessments showed the following attainment:

> 81 per cent at (or above) expected levels in Reading.
> 60 per cent at (or above) expected levels in Writing.
> 78 per cent at (or above) expected levels in Maths.

In addition, one fifth of the year group was assessed in maths at the end of Reception and again at the end of Year One, using the 'Sandwell' test. (These children comprised a complete range of abilities.) Of these children, half of them made more than 18 months of progress in the 12 month period (and half of those made more than two years' progress!) Only four of the children made less than a year of progress and in each case, we knew the exact reasons. (In each of these cases there was an event in their life that caused emotional turmoil – further evidence of the need to prioritise emotional well-being.)

All these numbers tell only a tiny part of the story. However, the qualitative data contained within the hundreds of photos and examples of events within this book, tell a much richer story. As stated, the vast majority of what has been done in Year One cannot be converted into numbers.

How do you quantify the progress made when a child perseveres for three months and then manages to travel across the complete run of monkey bars? How can we measure what impact that will have on a child going forward? Will they be more resilient? Will they have greater perseverance? Will they relish new challenges? None of these things is easy to measure, but they are vital life skills and must be valued.
How do you quantify the impact of so many events?

- holding a rabbit for the first time;
- planting, growing, picking and eating a strawberry;
- suddenly understanding why those four pieces of Numicon fit onto another piece;
- recognising the words in a cookery book;

Monkey bars and rope swings are the only fixed equipment that I would advocate. They are a superb way to develop hand and arm muscles – crucial for fine motor control.

- being able to swim across the pool;
- working together with a friend to build a model;
- seeing your teacher with her new baby;
- eating vegetables for the first time;
- building a perfect pyramid with the blocks;
- laughing with your friends;
- collecting eggs from the chicken coop;
- making a surfboard and surfing on the 'sea';
- managing to get the bulb to light with wires, batteries and clips;
- sewing some fabric and making a bag;
- creating a recipe, cooking it and tasting the results;
- using a drill for the first time at the woodwork bench.

This list could go on and on – just re-read this book to see the hundreds of experiences that the children have had – the impact of which it is almost impossible to measure. **We must trust that what engages children is right for them, even if we can't 'measure' its impact with numbers!**

Setting up the environment

Review and reflect

In this chapter, rather than describe any area of the environment, I will explain how the staff felt that the environment had worked, which areas need changing (if any) and what needs to be done before September.

If you have read the whole book, you will know that at the start of the year the children could only go in their own indoor classroom. This meant that we tried to have all areas of provision in each room and, where this was not possible, we had units

that could be moved around. So, for example, there were cooking and sewing units on wheels and the children could wheel them into whichever room they were needed. However, quite quickly the staff team decided that it would be better to create 'specialisms' within the rooms and this was trialled and very successful. It also meant that the children were **free-flowing between all three classrooms.** When this had been trialled in Reception, it had not worked for some of our most vulnerable children and therefore had not been continued. It does work very well in Reception, if there are just two classes, but with 90 children, it was very difficult. So, in July, the Year One classes have the following specialisms – Giraffe class has the creative area and resources, Rhino class has the science, history and geography resources and Gorilla class has the cooking area. As the end of year approaches, the staff have decided to leave the classes as they are now and trial free-flow between all the classes from September.

A constant complaint, amongst the Reception and Year One staff, is the lack of a cooker within the classes. The staff have to go to one of the dining rooms with anything that needs cooking. This has been discussed at senior leadership team meetings and there are plans to **create a permanent cooking area** in one of the prefabricated buildings in the outdoor area between Reception and Year One. Although not in the actual classroom, it will be accessible easily from the outdoor areas of both year groups – convenient and safe.

In many schools, class displays create huge amounts of work and stress. In terms of impact on learning, there is little evidence to show a clear causal link. I often wonder who the displays are for. In an effort to reduce workload, we keep **display boards** to

a minimum number and, where possible, make them accessible and useful. Therefore, one is used for learning journeys for the focus children each week, one is used for stories (waiting to be acted out), another is used to display current pieces of work and yet another contains support materials for the children to use when writing. In nursery and Reception, we have changed all the backing to hessian in an effort to 'calm' the environment and also to reduce workload (this backing should be permanent). The staff agreed that they would like this in Year One as well and so, during the last few weeks of the year, all the **boards were backed with hessian**. Several 'Easy Easel' bars (from Creative Cascade UK Ltd) are around the classrooms – making it

This till is from Ikea – it is also a solar powered calculator. Alex's number line is on the table – this is used as a record of which challenges have been completed. The staff have a hole punch and will 'clip' the number relating to the particular challenge.

The money belts are designed to be used by joggers. They can be purchased for about £2 each. Having seen how much learning has resulted from their use, it is definitely money well spent.

very simple to put learning journey sheets up and take them down – but also, as shown in the photo on page 200, useful for phonic cards, or key words that the children can take down, refer to and then replace with ease.

If you look at the November chapter, you will read about the introduction of the **money belts**. This has been very successful and will definitely be continued in September with the new cohort.

The 'logistics' for the organisation of the bags has developed over the year, with surprising 'side-benefits'. Each bag is now numbered and each child knows which bag is theirs. This enables the staff to differentiate the coins in the bags. For example,

Resources do not have to cost a lot of money. Old saucepans, such as the ones seen here, are appealing to children. They are real and usually much stronger than 'toy' saucepans.

by July the children have 50p to spend: some children will have a 50p coin, others will have 50 × 1p. At the end of each day, the children remove their money belt and a child is tasked with putting them out on a table in order from 1 – 30. Staff, or if there is time, some children, can then add the money to each belt, ready for the next day.

The **outdoor environment has worked exceptionally well**. Even on the very last day of term, the children were outside enjoying the environment, fully engaged in purposeful play. They are responsible for maintaining the environment too, and so there was no need to stop them from using the area at the end of the year. On the last day, they played, tidied and went home! Inevitably some areas needed re-stocking, for example, we needed to order some more sand, but the overall evaluation was extremely positive. One area that needed attention was the salt bin containing the fabric, which had been left open during a heavy downpour of rain and so the fabric was wet. In addition, there was nowhere for the water to escape and therefore the fabric at the bottom was completely saturated. We removed and discarded some of the material and then drilled several holes in the bottom of the salt bin to ensure future water could drain away.

Diary extracts: examples of development and learning

WHAT TO LOOK OUT FOR

- Children remain fully engaged in their learning.
- Assessments show good or outstanding progress.
- Parents express great satisfaction with the provision in Year One.
- The children know what to expect in Year Two and are looking forward to the journey.
- Staff are exhausted!

Harvest and eat!

The May chapter explains how the growing area can be developed over the period of the year. By July, many of the items can be harvested and it is essential that the children experience this part of the process, in order to fully appreciate what all the hard work has achieved. The children in the photo on the next page have picked strawberries and raspberries and have decided to make a fruit smoothie. Earlier in the year, they had done the same thing, but with fruit that they bought at the local shop. This smoothie is far more special and, no doubt tastier, because the children are fully aware of the effort it has taken to produce the fruit.

Young children don't always need to sit and write

Whenever I was in Year One this month, I did see the children doing focus tasks with an adult and these children were sitting at tables. However, the rest of the children were free-flowing and still lots of them were writing, but most were not sitting at a table and many were not indoors. Some were outside, some on their tummies on the ground, some standing at a table, others with clipboards, some sharing the writing on one piece of paper, or writing on the large whiteboards. As practitioners, we need to ensure that each child can operate in the way that suits them. We must remember that they are all unique, all different and all have their own way of doing things.

In this picture, even though there is a chair available, neither child has opted to sit on it.

Den building

One of the new challenges involved building a den for the lions. Over the period of a few weeks, the dens became more sophisticated and 'fit for purpose' as these pictures show. The need for a strong, waterproof roof led to design changes, then straw was added for comfort.

Escape!

One challenge brought surprising results. The children had to think about how they could escape if a lion was chasing them. Several ideas emerged, for example playing drums very loudly to scare the lion, or making traps. However, Jamie had the most original idea – make special glasses to become invisible! – simple!

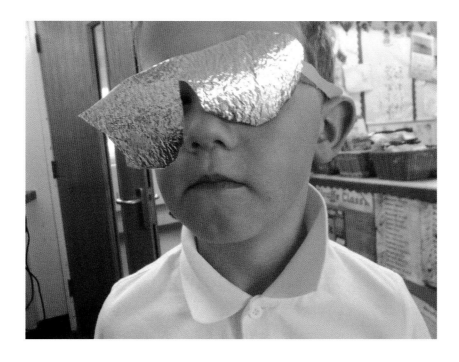

Woodwork skills develop

One of the challenges from the new book is to create an animal that lives on the Savannah. The photos below speak for themselves!

Other materials available

The clay has become a very popular medium. The concentration and clear enjoyment can be seen on Kevin's face. This demonstrates the level of care that is taken when a child selects to do something themselves.

As the term comes to an end, everyone is exhausted, but the sense of achievement is immense. The staff team in Year One have worked so hard to make the year a success. The learning support assistants have been completely committed to the process and, without this commitment, the learning and progress would not have been possible. The teachers took a 'leap of faith' to follow the ideas and systems to achieve their agreed vision, and the results have been superb. Ninety children engaged and learning through play in Year One. Something to shout about!

Conclusion

This photo shows a group of children, aged five and six, carrying out an experiment. They are all engaged and interested and, if we could scan their brains at this moment, we would see new synapses forming. These children are independent, curious, energetic, enthusiastic, happy, creative, confident and resilient. They are taking risks, interacting, collaborating, persevering and solving problems. If you ask any teacher what characteristics support learning, they would list just these attributes and behaviours. These children love learning, just as they did when they were born, just as they did in nursery and in Reception. No one has told them to do this experiment, they have chosen to do it because it interests them. This **self-motivation is a powerful driver** and yet, in most schools, it is being overlooked. In most schools, the children in Year One are controlled and directed by adults, with numerous rewards and sanctions in place to achieve compliance. The children in this photo are not expecting any reward for doing this activity, nor would there be any sanction if they chose not to do it. They have the freedom to learn about whatever interests them and through whatever vehicle they choose. We know that the **interest will deliver engagement** and then the children will challenge and push themselves further than if we dictate the content. **The best education is one that teaches children *how to learn*.** Content-driven education systems teach children to do as they are told.

At Carterhatch Infant School, we have 90 children in Year One and it is an immense task to ensure that they all have the freedom to learn in the way that suits them as unique individuals. We have also had to ensure that time is made available to teach the children the literacy and mathematical skills that they need in order to be able to learn about what interests them. However, we are absolutely clear that **literacy and maths are tools to facilitate learning**, they are not an end in themselves. As stated in the introduction, it is a tragedy that, for many young children, the curriculum has been narrowed to virtually nothing but literacy and maths. We have a fear-driven culture in education at the moment. Head teachers are terrified to take risks in case their results dip and they end up losing their jobs. However, as this book shows, it is by doing what is best for the children – by delivering an education that interests and engages them – that the best results can be achieved.

The staff team have an agreed vision and this is kept in mind at all times. The vision for Year One includes a wish to tap into the children's natural desire to learn, giving them control of their learning, with an emphasis on collaborative learning and constant use of the outdoors. This vision is based on the knowledge that children want to learn, but they each want to learn in their own unique way. We have 90 children who are all unique and yet they all want to learn.

> **'Play' is anything that a child does in order to satisfy their desire to learn.**

Let's stop being afraid of using the word 'play' but let's be clear that it is the most powerful vehicle for learning. If we allow the children to play with whatever they choose and in the way that they choose, we are removing stress from the education process. We do not have to coerce children to work, nor do we need to reward children for doing their 'work' because **their 'work' is their 'play' and they will do it relentlessly**. The challenge is to ensure that the play is truly engaging and not at a level which just keeps children 'occupied'. The measure of this is the levels of involvement that are described in the Introduction. We do not just want our children to be occupied, we want them deeply engaged in their play, as that is when we know they are learning and progressing.

This book explains the logistics and practicalities in detail but **the vision must be the starting point** if you are thinking about developing your practice. You need to be absolutely clear about why you want to do things differently and what your vision is for the children. We know from our own experiences in life that the things that engage us are the things that we will persevere with, they are the things that we always make time for and always have energy for. It is the same with children, so our vision must be to deliver an education that **engages** children. In creating a vision for your children, start from the child, start by asking what will engage a five year old. Is it more engaging to learn about weight using cubes or by making a cake? Is it more engaging to learn about list writing by writing in a literacy book or by writing on a piece of paper and going to the shop? Is it more engaging to learn about the seasons by completing a worksheet or by playing outside in all weathers? In each case the engagement means that the child will engage with the learning willingly. It also means that the learning will be deep and meaningful and far more likely to be remembered and to have long-term impact. These are the reasons we need to use when trying to persuade people about the advantages of play-based, child-led, hands-on learning.

The book also explains the planning and paperwork that we have devised (and which is now being used in hundreds of schools) to support this way of working. The main message is that deepest engagement happens when **children choose what to do** and how to do it. **This cannot be pre-planned**, because we do not know what any child will choose to do. Therefore, our staff observe the children constantly, looking for moments when they can add something, they decide what to do (this is planning) and they 'teach' the next step immediately. We call this '**planning in the moment**'. Some of these interactions are recorded afterwards as a record of the teaching and learning that has taken place.

To achieve the highest levels of involvement, experience has shown me that the practice needs to offer the children:

- security, by prioritising emotional well-being;
- trust, that they want to learn in their own unique way;
- friendships;
- trusting relationships with adults;
- independence;
- risk;
- autonomy;
- excitement and laughter;
- responsibility;
- first-hand experiences;
- long periods of uninterrupted time;
- freedom to be outdoors or indoors;
- resources that are open-ended (i.e. they can be used in a million different ways);
- **skilled teaching – i.e. timely and appropriate to the individual** (including facilitating, supporting, modelling, suggesting, encouraging, narrating, demonstrating, explaining, providing resources, etc.).

This is not an easy option. It is complex and exhausting but has the potential to be amazing, as this book has shown. Be brave, be persuasive, be a champion for our children, cause a stir, do what is right for the children – let them take the lead – trust that they want to learn – and let them play!

Appendix A: Ferre Laevers' levels of involvement

Involvement focuses on the extent to which pupils are operating to their full capabilities. In particular it refers to whether the child is focused, engaged and interested in various activities.

The Leuven Scale for Involvement specifies:

1 Low activity
   Activity at this level can be simple, stereotypic, repetitive and passive. The child is absent and displays no energy. There is an absence of cognitive demand. The child characteristically may stare into space. N.B. This may be a sign of inner concentration.

2 A frequently interrupted activity
   The child is engaged in an activity but half of the observed period includes moments of non-activity, in which the child is not concentrating and is staring into space. There may be frequent interruptions in the child's concentration, but his/her involvement is not enough to return to the activity.

3 Mainly continuous activity
   The child is busy at an activity but it is at a routine level and the real signals for involvement are missing. There is some progress but energy is lacking and concentration is at a routine level. The child can be easily distracted.

4 Continuous activity with intense moments
   The child's activity has intense moments during which activities at Level 3 can come to have special meaning. Level 4 is reserved for the kind of activity seen in those intense moments, and can be deduced from the 'Involvement signals'. This level of activity is resumed after interruptions. Stimuli, from the surrounding environment, however attractive cannot seduce the child away from the activity.

5 Sustained intense activity
   The child shows continuous and intense activity revealing the greatest involvement. In the observed period not all the signals for involvement need to be there, but the essential ones must be present: concentration, creativity, energy and persistence. This intensity must be present for almost all the observation period.

Level of involvement

Time	Involvement	Comments
Average		

Appendix B: Cooking design sheet

Name _____ Date _____

I am going to make _____

Ingredients	Design
1. _____	
2. _____	
3. _____	
4. _____	
5. _____	
6. _____	
7. _____	

Method

1. _____

2. _____

3. _____

4. _____

5. _____

6. _____

7. _____

8. _____

Photo of finished product

Evaluation

Appendix C: Autumn Term focus child letter

Planning for your child's learning journey

Next week we will be focusing on _____. We will be observing them while they play to find out more about their interests and how they are progressing.

We value the knowledge and understanding you have of your child and would really appreciate it if you would share this with us so that together we can plan activities to meet your child's needs. This will help us plan for their future learning and development.

Is there anything significant happening in your child's life at the moment e.g. visits, holidays, new pets, family celebrations?
Do you have anything you would like to ask us about your child's progress and development?
We will be focusing on: 1.   2.   3.

Please could your child bring any of the following items to school to show to the class:

Baby clothes	Favourite food packets
Favourite toy	Tickets
Family photos	Any items that tell us about your child and family

Please could you return this sheet with the items by _____

Appendix D: Learning journey

Year One Learning Journey For .... Date ....

Identified Areas For Focus:	PSE, RE
General/Parents:	**I imagine:**- Literacy, design and technology, art and design, music, PE
Curriculum:	**I understand:**- Numeracy, science, history, geography, computing
*	Consultation Meeting
*	
*	

Identified Areas For Future Focus:

Cake Recipe

You can use

1 egg or

2 eggs or 3 eggs or

4 eggs or 5 eggs or 6 eggs

More eggs = bigger cake!

Balance the eggs with the flour.

Put the flour in the bowl.

~ 1 ~

Balance the eggs with the sugar.

Put the sugar in the bowl.

Balance the eggs with the butter.

Put the butter in the bowl.

~ 3 ~

Add the eggs to the bowl.

Mix, mix, mix!

~ 4 ~

Put the mixture in a baking tin.

Cook at 180°C for 15 minutes.

Decorate your cake and eat it!

Appendix F: Story scribing

- Sit beside the child (if you are right handed, put the child on your left).
- Make sure the child watches you write (i.e. the paper should be in front of the child if possible). Write exactly what the child says.
- Use your knowledge of each child to decide which teaching is appropriate.
- Say the words as you write them.
- Sometimes stop and read what you have written and then let the child carry on.
- Sound out some words as you write them.
- Point out spaces, capitals and full stops, etc.
- Exaggerate some letter formation.
- Ask the child to sound out some words for you.
- Ask the child to write a few letters – or words – as appropriate to the individual child.
- Use terms such as 'characters', 'author', etc.
- The **story** is the important part – keep the momentum – the teaching should not slow down the scribing too much.

Anna Ephgrave

Appendix G: Story map

Name _____ Date _____

Title_____

Characters:

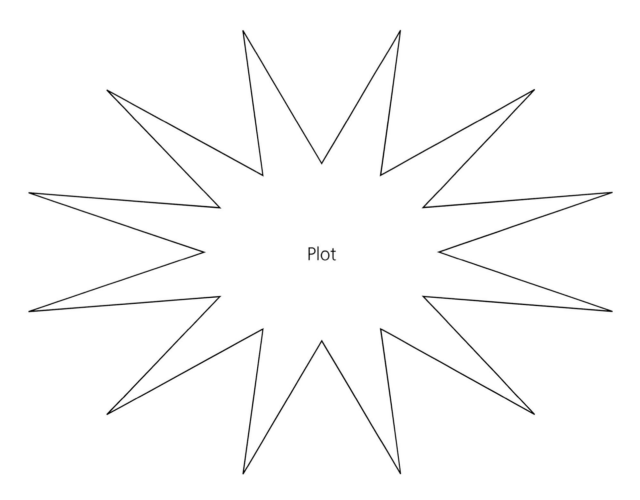

Plot

Setting:

Appendix H: Woodwork design sheet

Name _____ Date _____

I am going to make _____

Design

Materials and tools	
1. _____	4. _____
2. _____	5. _____
3. _____	6. _____

Photo of finished piece	Evaluation
	☺ ☹

Appendix I: Suppliers

www.creativecascade.co.uk – for Creative Cascade Sets, welly storage, woodwork benches and Funky Fountains (products designed by Anna!). Also offers advice and practical support for environment make-overs – both indoors and outdoors.

Skips, ditches, parents (great suppliers of 'junk modelling' resources), charity shops, etc.

DIY stores and online companies – for ropes, marine plywood, pulleys, woodwork tools and elasticated rope.

www.communityplaythings.co.uk – for wooden blocks (various sizes) and storage units.

www.costco.co.uk – for heavy duty tarpaulins and shelving.

www.cosydirect.com – for open-ended resources at reasonable prices.

www.ikea.co.uk – for storage units, canopies and children's furniture.

www.impbins.com – for salt bins.

www.olympicgymnasium.com – for A-frames and ladders etc. Look in their 'nursery' section.

www.pvc-strip.co.uk – for plastic strips to hang in doorways.

www.shedstore.co.uk – for sheds (Model: Larchlap Overlap Maxi Wallstore 63 is useful for storing large wooden blocks).

www.earlyexcellence.com – for open shelving in particular.

www.filplastic.co.uk – for shopping baskets.

www.freedomtolearn.co.uk – offers support, consultancy and training based around the ideas in this book.

Appendix J: Spring Term focus child letter

Carterhatch

Infant School • Children's Centres

Next week we will be focusing on _____. We will be working with them to find out more about how they learn best, their interests and how they are progressing.

We value the knowledge and understanding you have of your child and hope that we can work together to support their development.

Is there anything significant happening in your child's life at the moment e.g. visits, holidays, new pets, family celebrations?
Do you have anything you would like to ask us about your child's progress and development?
At school this week, your child will be wearing a watch. Please help them look at clocks at home. Please could you help them complete these clocks.

Dinner time   Bed time   Breakfast time

Please could you email a few photos of your home and family to year1@carterhatch-inf.enfield.sch.uk

Appendix K: Science design sheet

Name _____ Date _____

I will be testing _____

Prediction _____

_____

_____

_____

Equipment	Photo
1. _____	
2. _____	
3. _____	
4. _____	

Method

1. _____

2. _____

3. _____

4. _____

Evaluation	☺	☹

Appendix L: Report sheet

Name: _____ Week commencing: _____

In English I can:	Photos
★	
★	
★	
Next I need to learn:	
●	
In Maths I can:	
★	
★	
★	
Next I need to learn:	
●	

In other areas I demonstrate:

Curiosity, imagination, initiative, determination, perseverance, risk-taking, energy, fascination, attention to detail, resilience, enjoyment of challenge, pride, problem solving ability, ability to plan ahead, flexibility, co-operation

This week I have been learning about . . .	

Appendix M: Creative design sheet

Name _____ Date _____

I am going to make _____

Design

Materials and tools	
1. _____	4. _____
2. _____	5. _____
3. _____	6. _____

Photo of finished piece	Evaluation
	🙂
	☹

Bibliography

Athey, C. 1990. *Extending Thought in Young Children: A Parent-Teacher Partnership.* Paul Chapman Publishing Ltd. London.

Bilton, H. 2010. *Outdoor Learning in the Early Years.* Routledge. Oxfordshire.

Bowlby, J. 1997. *Attachment and Loss.* Pimlico. London.

Brooker, L. 2002. *Starting School.* Oxford University Press. Oxford.

Bruce, T. 2005. *Early Childhood Education.* 3rd Edition. Hodder and Stoughton. London.

Bruce, T. 2001. *Learning Through Play: Babies, Toddlers and the Foundation Years.* Hodder Arnold. London.

Dyer, W. 2007. *Mercury's Child.* Booklocker.com, Inc. for Colly and Sons UK.

Ephgrave, A. 2012. *The Reception Year in Action.* 2nd Edition. Routledge. Oxfordshire.

Ephgrave, A. 2015. *The Nursery Year in Action.* Routledge. Oxfordshire.

Fisher, J. 2002. *Starting From The Child.* 2nd Edition. Open University Press. Maidenhead.

Gerhardt, S. 2004. *Why Love Matters.* Routledge. Hove.

Gray. P. 2013. *Free to Learn.* Basic Books. New York.

Greenfield, S. 2014. *Mind Change.* Rider. London.

Gussin-Paley, V. 1991. *The Boy Who Would Be A Helicopter.* Harvard University Press. Cambridge, MA.

Isaacs, S. 1966. *Intellectual Growth in Young Children.* Shockern Books. New York.

Isaacs, S. 1929. *The Nursery Years.* Routledge & Kegan Paul. London.

Laevers, F. 1994. *Five Levels of Well-Being.* Leuven University Press. Belgium.

Legerstee, M., Haley, D. & Bornstein, M. 2013. *The Infant Mind.* The Guilford Press. New York.

Nutbrown, C. 2006. *Threads of Thinking.* 3rd Edition. Sage. London.

Pellegrini, A.D. 2011. *The Oxford Handbook of the Development of Play.* Oxford University Press. Oxford.

Read, V. & Hughes, A. 2009. *Developing Attachment in Early Years Settings.* David Fulton Publishers. Oxfordshire.

Robinson, D. & Groves, J. 2002. *Introducing Bertrand Russell.* Icon Books. Cambridge.

Robinson, K. & Aronica, L. 2015. *Creative Schools.* Viking Penguin. New York.

Rose, J. and Rogers, S. 2012. *The Role of the Adult in Early Years Settings.* Open University Press. New York.

Russell, D. 1932. *In Defence of Children.* Hamish Hamilton. London.

Solly, K. 2014. *Risk, Challenge and Adventure in the Early Years.* Routledge. Oxfordshire.

Vygotsky, L.S. 1987. *Mind in Society.* Harvard University Press. Cambridge, MA.

Whalley, M. 2007. *Involving Parents in their Children's Learning.* 2nd Edition. Paul Chapman Publishing. London.

Index